Mel Bay and Warner Bros. Publications Present..

JAZZ Guitar Standards

MW00804571

A Complete Approach to Playing Tunes...... II

- Lead Sheet

- Chord Melody Solo

- Comping Backup

- Single-Line Improvisation

Visit us on the Web at www.melbay.com • E-mail us at email@melbay.com

Introduction

Jazz Guitar Standards vol. II: A Complete Approach to Playing Tunes presents twenty-two classic jazz standards in the three formats jazz guitarists are usually required to master. Along with a lead sheet, etudes and arrangements for chord solos, comping, and single-note solos have been written by some of the best guitar arrangers and educators in the business. Because many arrangers were used for this project, the nomenclature has not been standardized. This will allow students to see many different ways of notating and naming chords. This will give students exposure to the different ways jazz arrangements can be written. Have fun mastering these great tunes.

One side note: there may be cases where the arranger choose to alter the key of a tune for the chord solo arrangement (see Jack Wilkins arrangement to "Long Ago and Far Away"). This change of key for the chord solo arrangement facilitates certain chord voicings that in some cases utilize open strings and sounds that are idiomatic to the guitar. The single-note solos and comping etudes have been kept in the same key as the lead sheet.

Lead Sheet Chords

Main and Alternate Substitution Labeling: The chord symbols found directly above the melody line are what we consider the **main** chords. These chord choices are derived from either original changes found in the most reliable piano/vocal sources, from the most famous recorded sources, from notes or arrangements by the composers themselves, or from the most commonly known renditions typically played by professional musicians. We have also provided some **alternate substitutions,** which are shown in parentheses above the **main** symbols. These changes are derived from either selected popular recordings by artists highly identified with a particular song or are based on common alternate renderings. These chords are optional and may be either played in place of or in conjunction with the **main** symbols. Notice that these chords will last as long as the main symbols or until the closing parenthesis is indicated.

Contents

All of You

Music and Lyrics by
COLE PORTER

ALL OF YOU

Arr. by Barry Greene

(Chord Melody)

Music and Lyrics by
Cole Porter

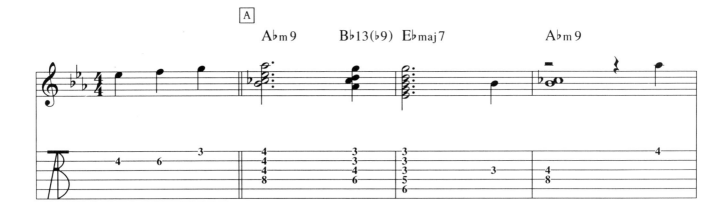

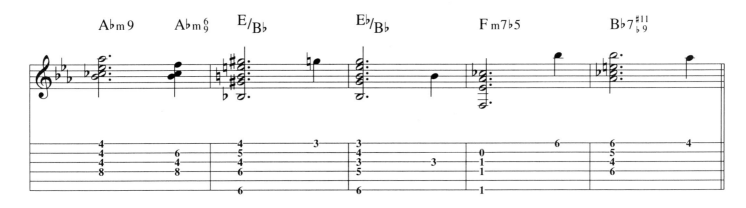

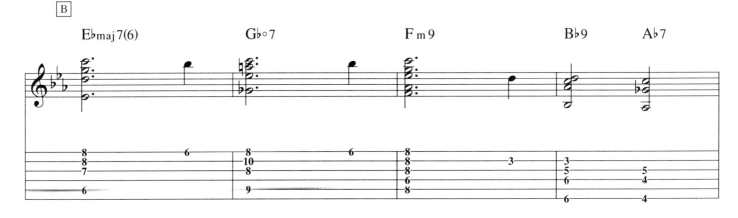

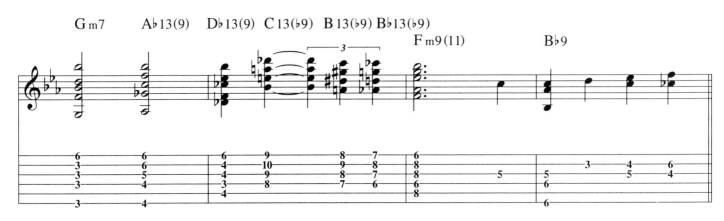

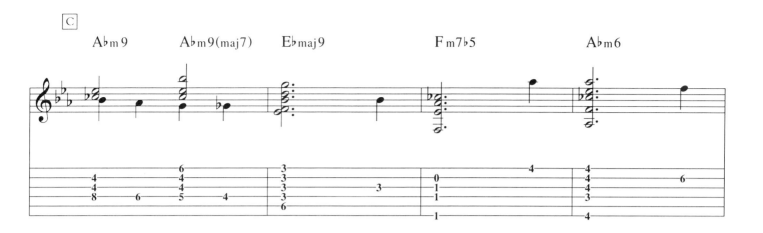

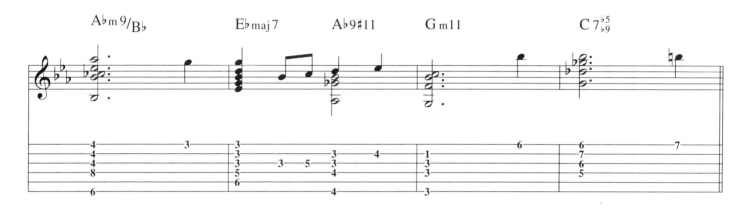

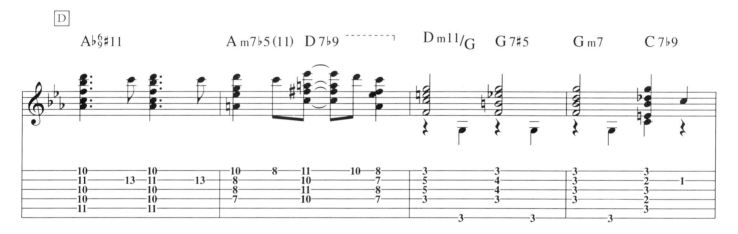

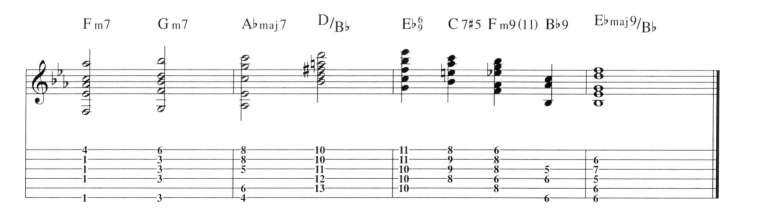

9

ALL OF YOU
(Comping Etude)

Arr. by Barry Greene

Music and Lyrics by
Cole Porter

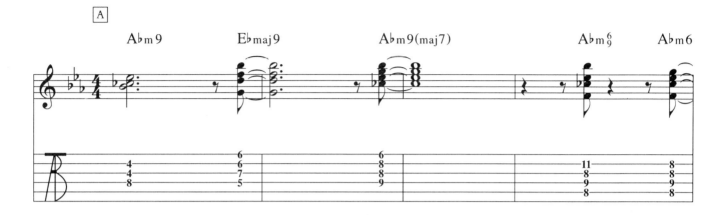

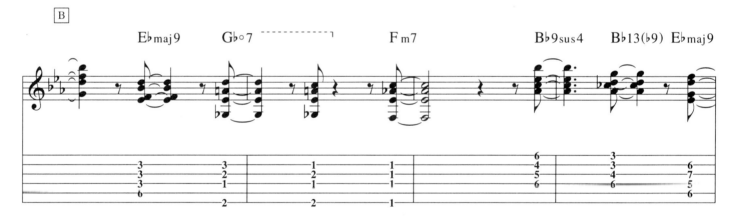

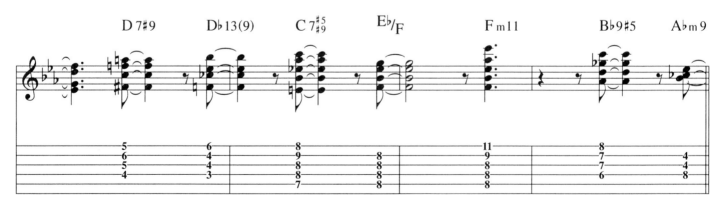

All of You
(Single-Note Solo)

Arr. by Barry Greene

Music and Lyrics by
Cole Porter

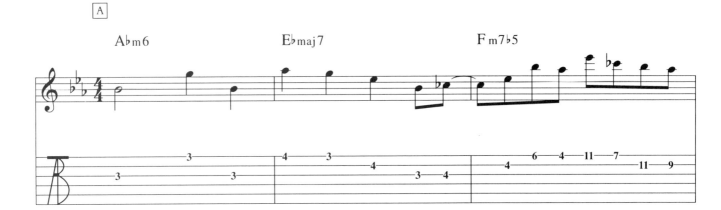

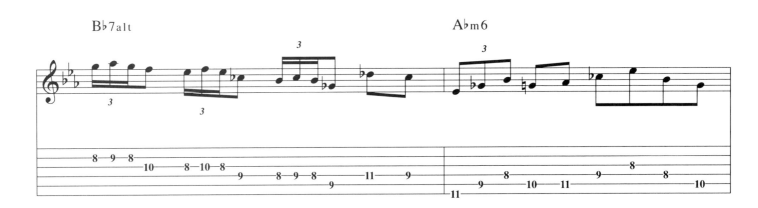

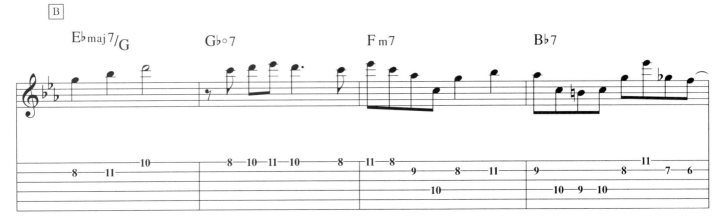

April In Paris

Words by E.Y. Harburg
Music by Vernon Duke

A-pril in Par-is, chest-nuts in blos-som, hol-i-day tab-les un-der the trees.

Ap-ril in Par-is, this is a feel-ing no one can ev-er re - - prise.

I nev-er knew the charm of Spring, nev-er met it face to face. I nev-er knew my heart could sing, nev-er miss'd a warm em - brace, till....

A-pril in Par-is; whom can I run to, what have you done to my heart?

April In Paris

(Chord Melody)

Arr. by Chris Buzzelli

Words by E.Y. Harburg
Music by Vernon Duke

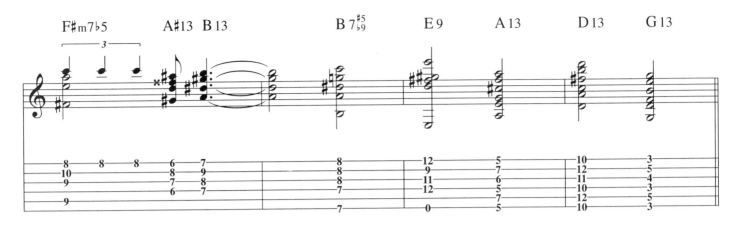

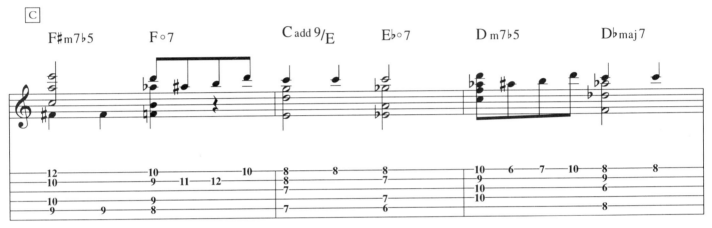

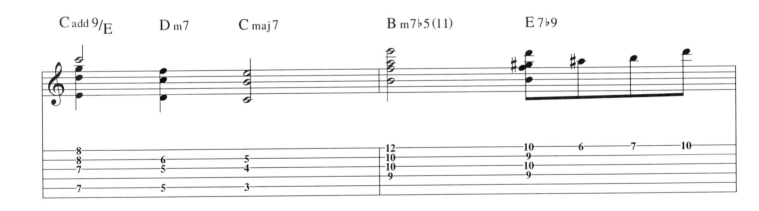

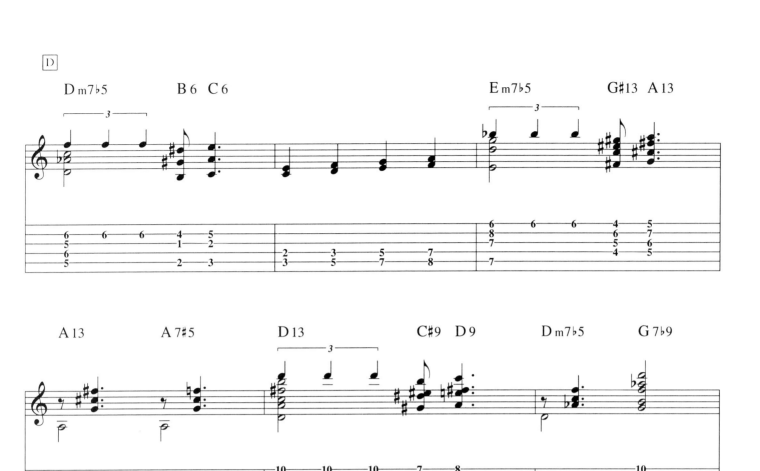

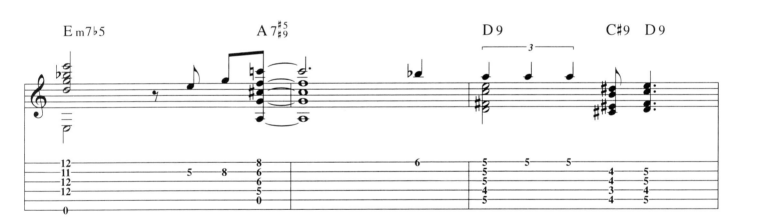

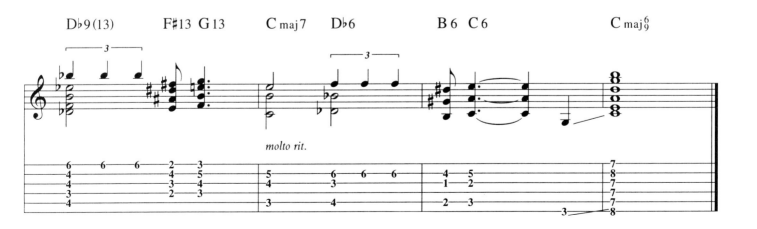

April In Paris

(Comping Etude)

Arr. by Chris Buzzelli

Words by E.Y. Harburg
Music by Vernon Duke

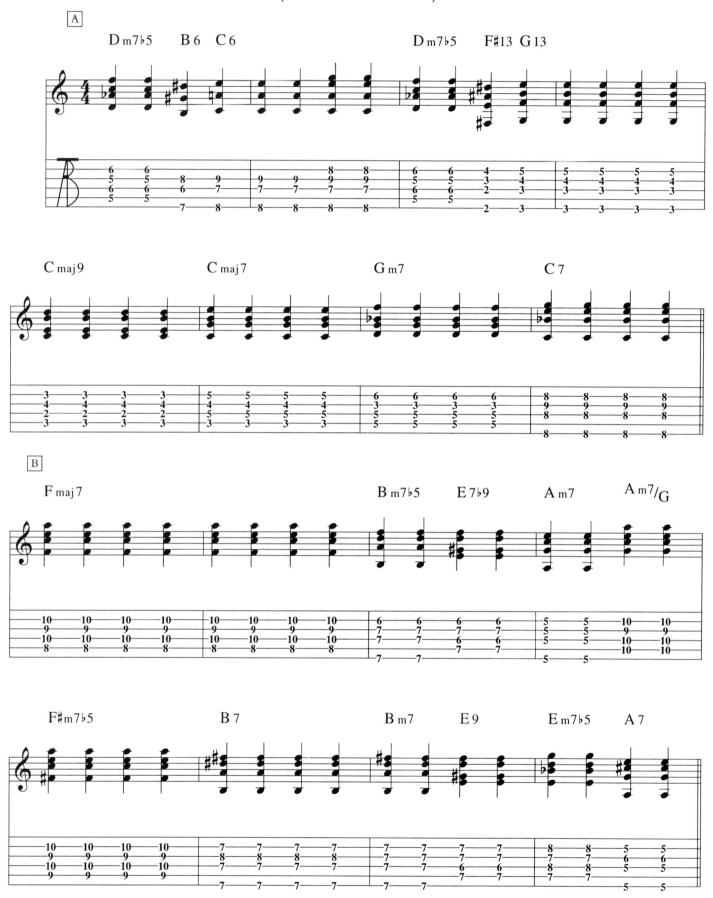

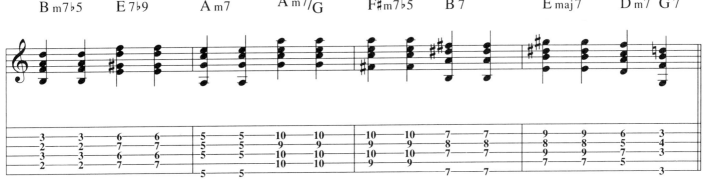

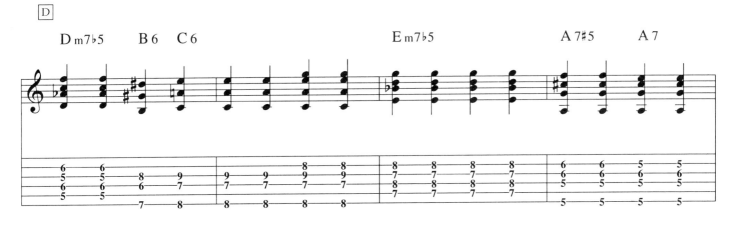

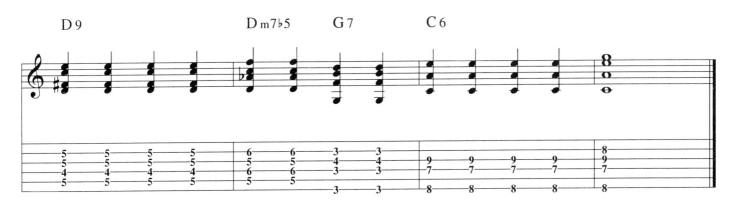

19

April In Paris

(Single-Note Solo)

Arr. by Chris Buzzelli

Words by E.Y. Harburg
Music by Vernon Duke

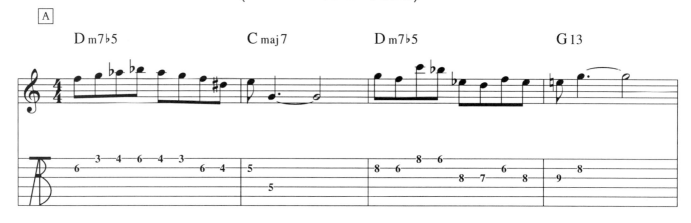

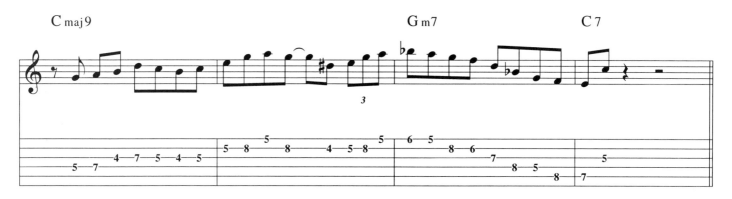

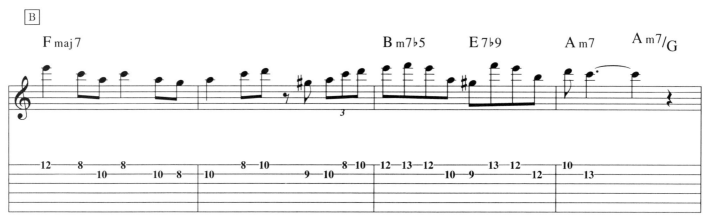

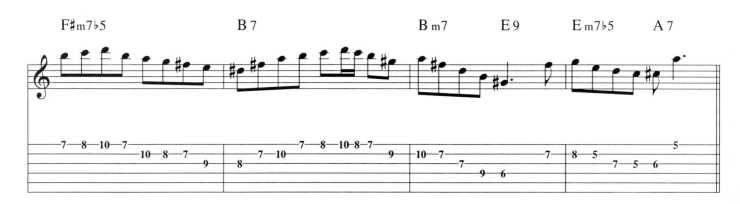

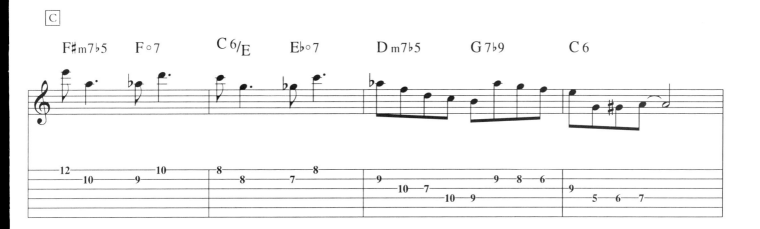

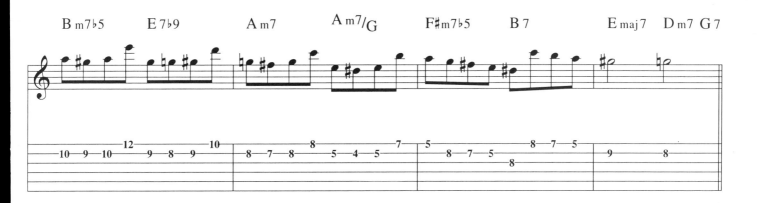

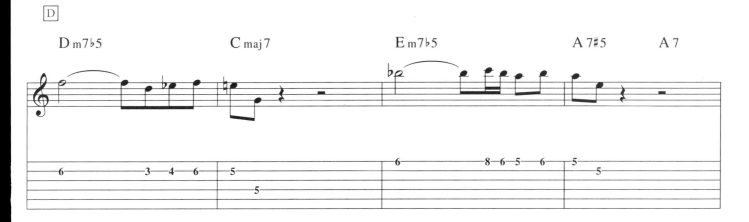

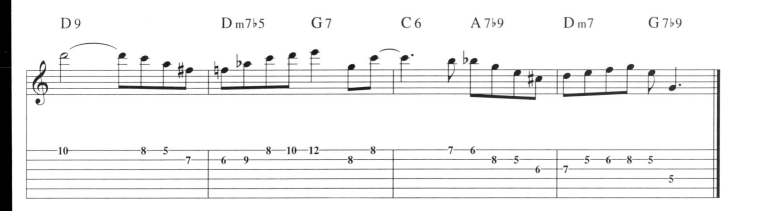

As Time Goes By

Words and Music by
Herman Hupfeld

Verse
Freely or Ballad

This day and age we're liv-ing in gives cause for ap-re-hen-sion, with speed and new in-ven-tion, and

things like third di-men-sion. Yet, we grow a tri-fle wear-y, with Mis-ter Ein-stein's the-'ry, so we

must get down to earth, at times re-lax, re-lieve the ten-sion. No mat-ter what the pro-gress or

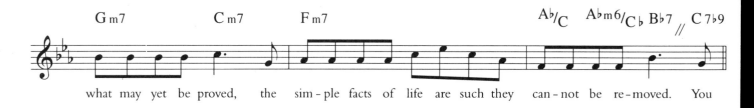

what may yet be proved, the sim-ple facts of life are such they can-not be re-moved. You

must re-mem-ber this, a kiss is still a kiss, a sigh is just a sigh;
when two lov-ers woo, they still say, 'I love you,' on that you can re-ly;

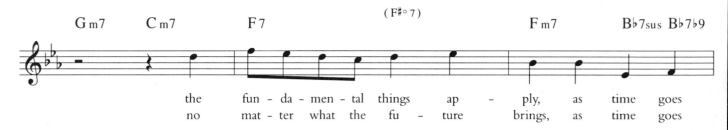

the fun-da-men-tal things ap - ply, as time goes
no mat-ter what the fu - ture brings, as time goes

As Time Goes By

Arr. by Dave Frackenpohl

(Chord Melody)

Words and Music by
Herman Hupfeld

Verse

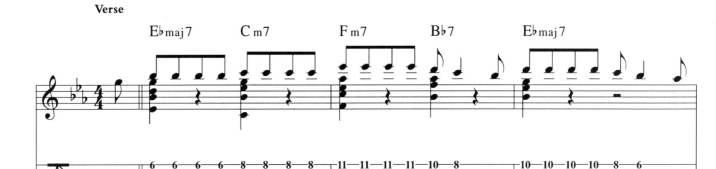

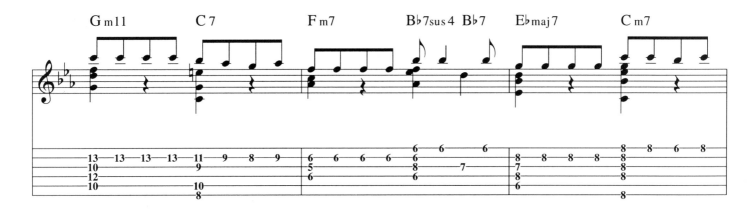

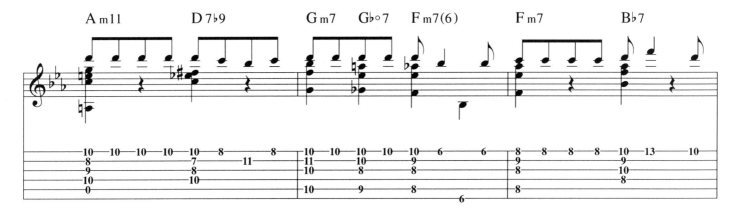

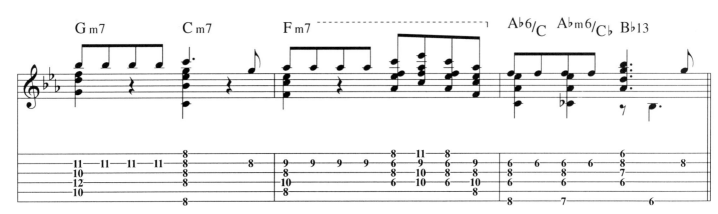

As Time Goes By
(Comping Etude)

Arr. by Dave Frackenpohl

Words and Music by
Herman Hupfeld

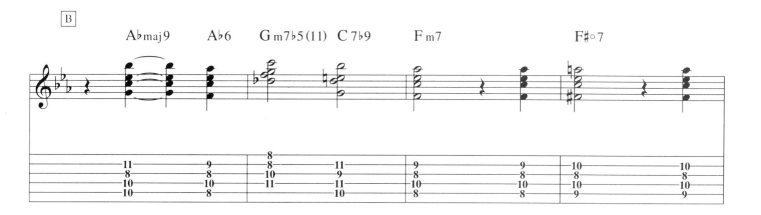

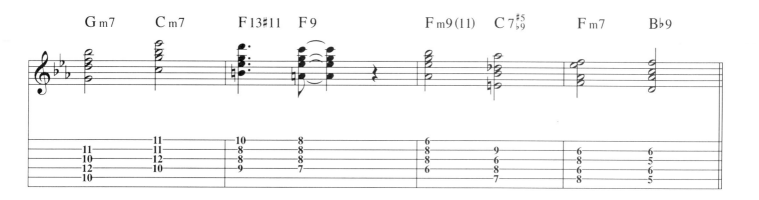

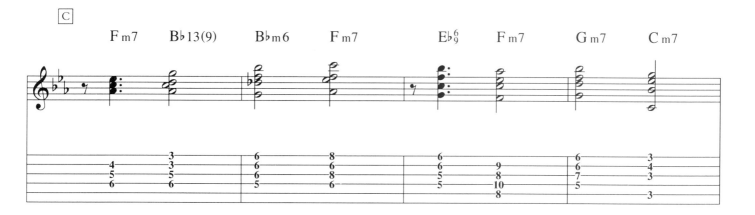

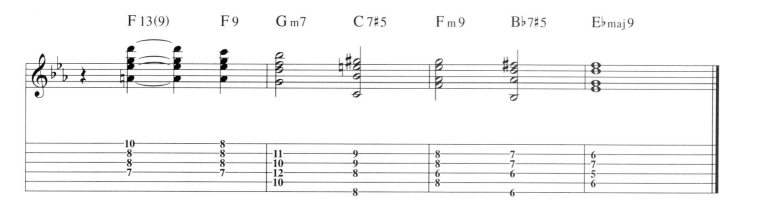

As Time Goes By
(Single-Note Solo)

Arr. by Dave Frackenpohl

Words and Music by
Herman Hupfeld

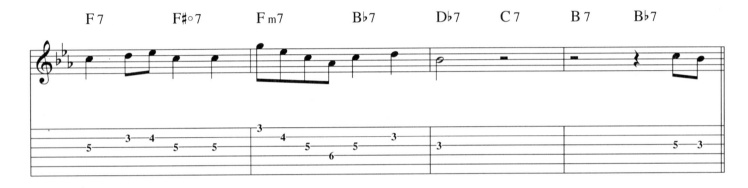

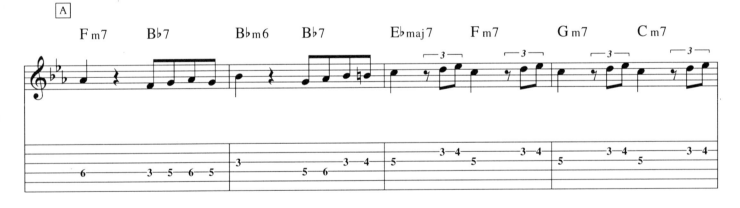

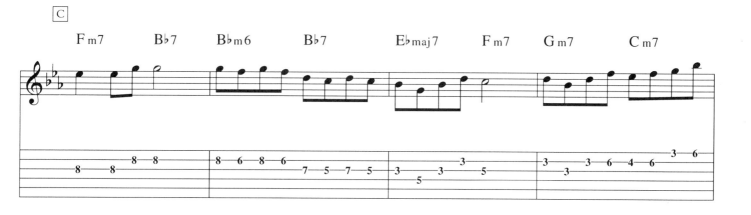

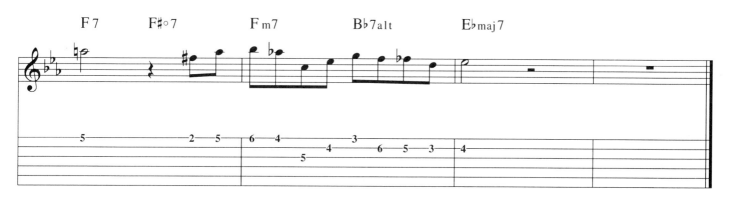

Bluesette

Words by NORMAN GIMBEL
Music by JEAN THIELEMANS

A

Medium Jazz Waltz

Bbmaj7   Am7b5   D7b9   Gm7

1. Poor lit-tle sad lit-tle blue blues-ette. Don't you
2. 3. Long as there's love in your heart to share, dear Blue-

C7b9   Fm7   Bb7   Ebmaj7   (Eb6)   Ebm7

cry, don't you fret. You can bet one luck-y day you'll
sette, don't des-pair. Some blue boy is long-ing, just like

Ab9   Dbmaj7   Dbm7   Gb9   **To Coda**   Cbmaj7

wak-en and your blues will be for-sak-en. One luck-y
you, to find a some-one to be true to; two lov-ing

Cm7b5   F9   Dm7   (G7#5#9) Db7   Cm7   (F7#5#9) F7

day love-ly love will come your way._____
arms he can nes-tle in and stay._____

B

Bbmaj7   Am7b5   D7b9   Gm7

Get set, blues-ette, true love is com-ing. Your trou-bled

C9   Fm7   Bb7   Ebmaj7   (Eb6)

heart soon will be hum-ming. *(Scat)*

Ebm7   Ab7   Dbmaj7   Dbm7

Gb9   Cbmaj7   Cm7b5

Doo-ya, doo-ya, doo-ya, doo-ya, doo-ya, doo-ya, doo-oo-

BLUESETTE

(CHORD MELODY)

Arr. by Dave Frackenpohl

Words by Norman Gimbel
Music by Jean Thielemans

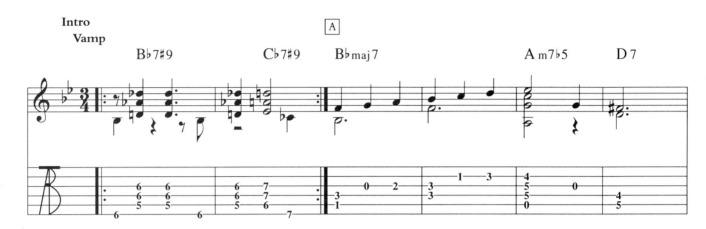

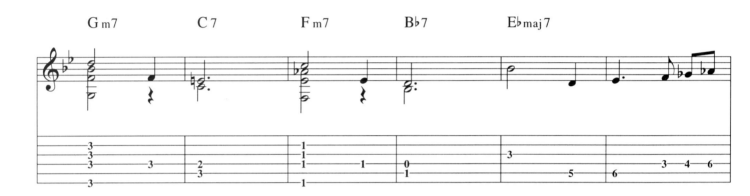

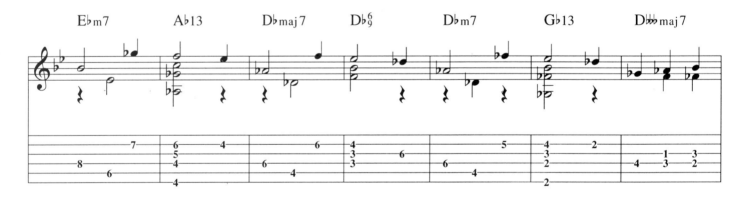

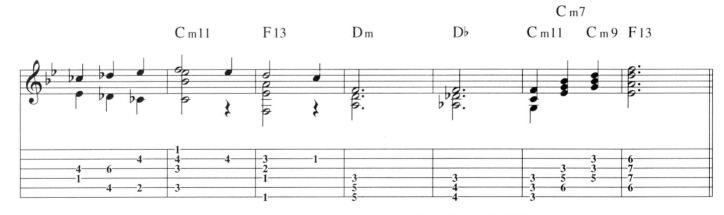

Bluesette
(Comping Etude)

Arr. by Dave Frackenpohl

Words by Norman Gimbel
Music by Jean Thielemans

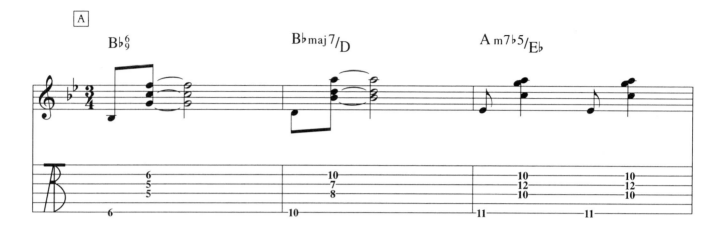

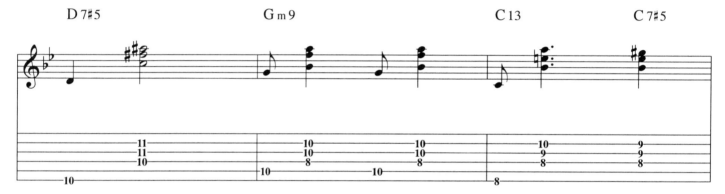

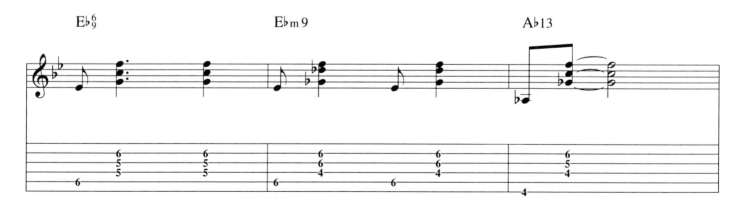

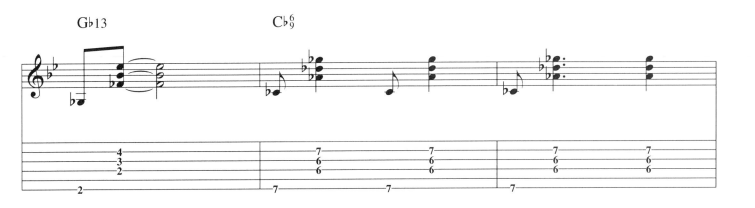

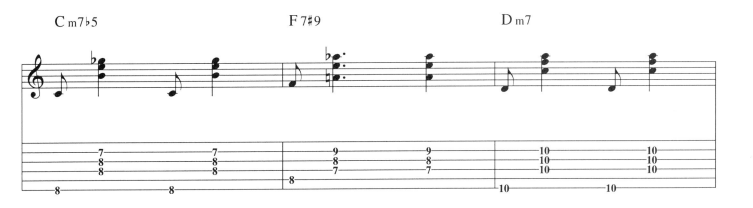

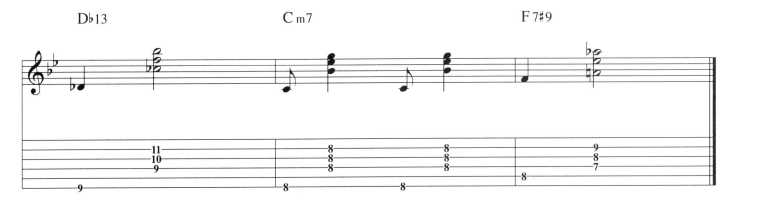

Bluesette
(Single-Note Solo)

Arr. by Dave Frackenpohl

Words by Norman Gimbel
Music by Jean Thielemans

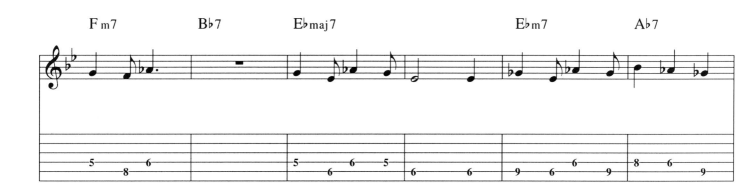

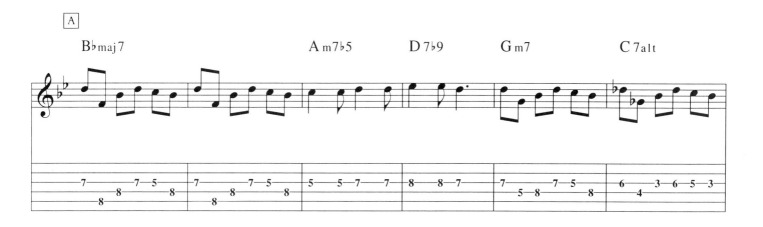

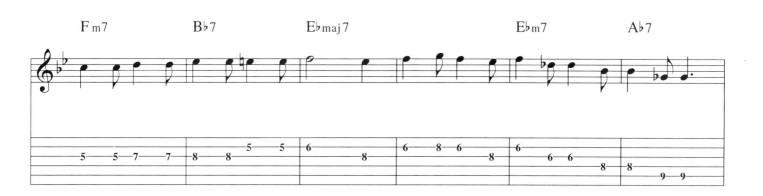

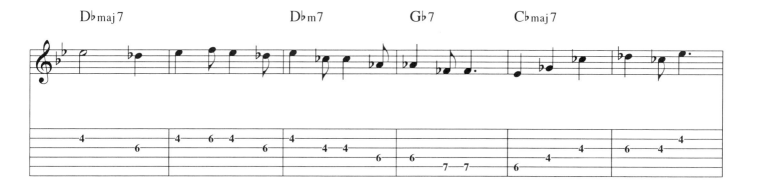

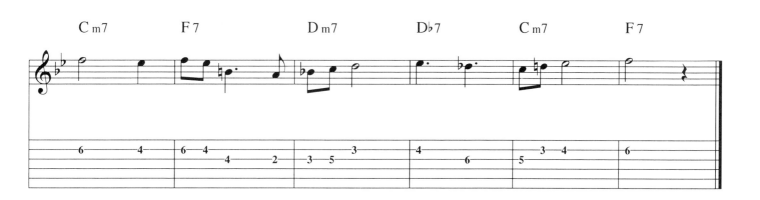

41

BUT NOT FOR ME

Music and Lyrics by
GEORGE GERSHWIN
and IRA GERSHWIN

BUT NOT FOR ME

(Chord Melody)

Arr. by Barry Greene

Music and Lyrics by
George Gershwin
and Ira Gershwin

But Not For Me
(Comping Etude)

Arr. by Barry Greene

Music and Lyrics by
George Gershwin
and Ira Gershwin

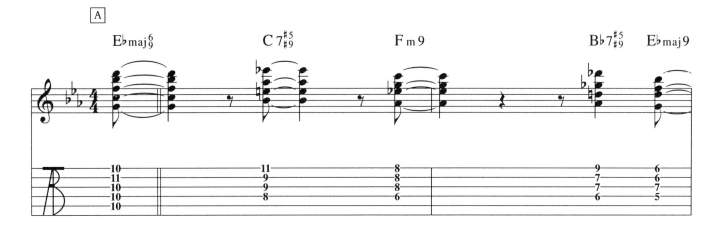

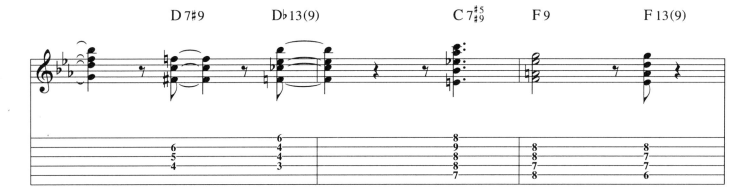

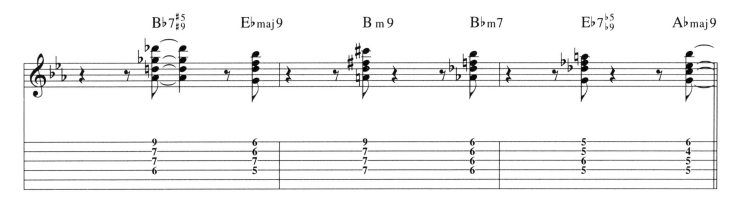

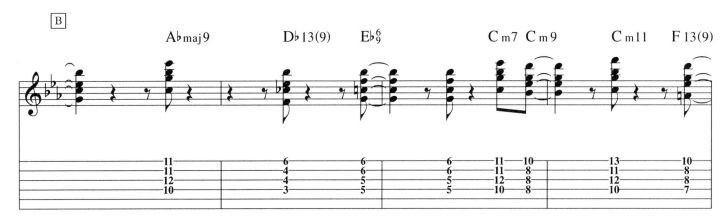

But Not For Me

(Single-Note Solo)

Arr. by Barry Greene

Music and Lyrics by
George Gershwin
and Ira Gershwin

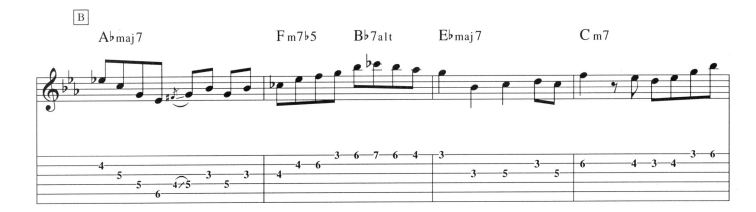

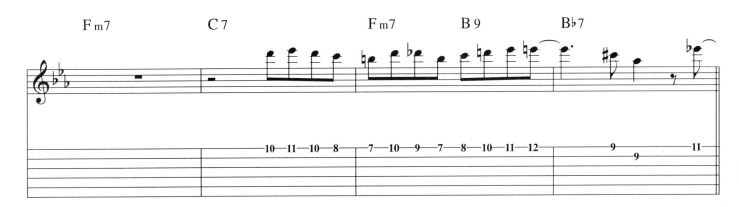

Can't Help Lovin' Dat Man

Music by Jerome Kern
Words by Oscar Hammerstein II

Can't Help Lovin' Dat Man

(CHORD MELODY)

Arr. by Ron Berman

Music by Jerome Kern
Words by Oscar Hammerstein II

A

Eb | Cm7 | Fm9 | Bb13

Eb maj7 | Cm7 | Ab maj7 | Ab m6 | Gm7 | Cm7

B7/A | Bb7#5 | Bb7b9 | Eb maj7/Bb | Cm11 | Fm9(11)/Ab | Bb9sus4 | Bb9#11

A

Eb | Cm7 | Fm7 | Bb9 | Bb7b9 | Eb | Cm

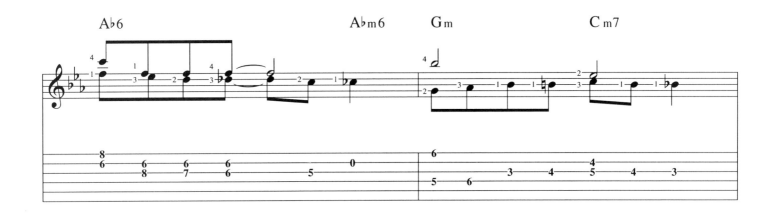

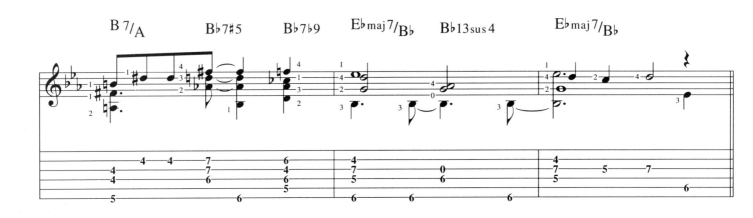

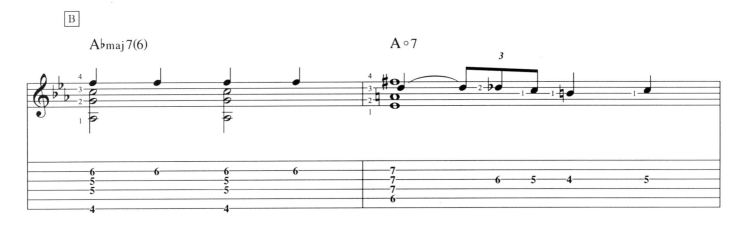

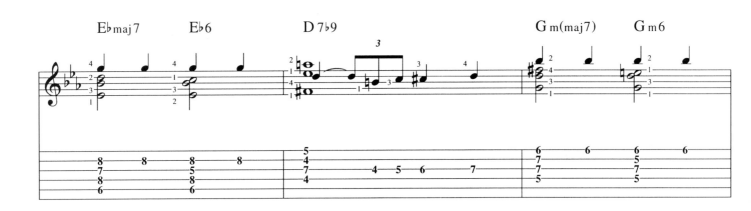

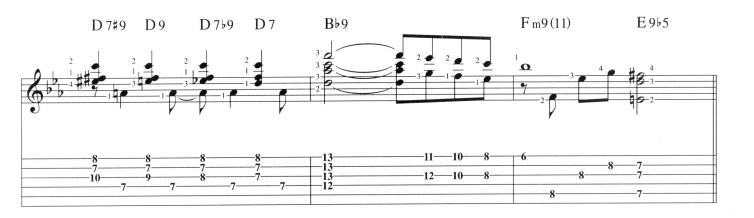

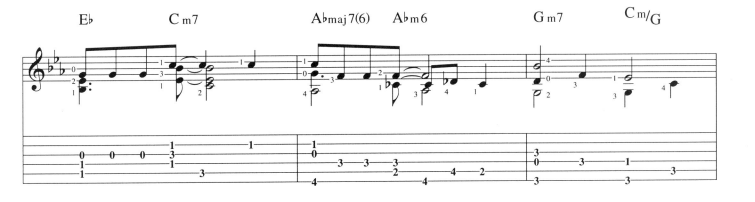

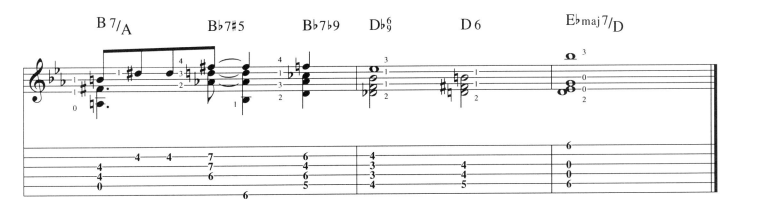

CAN'T HELP LOVIN' DAT MAN

Arr. by Ron Berman

(COMPING ETUDE)

Music by Jerome Kern
Words by Oscar Hammerstein II

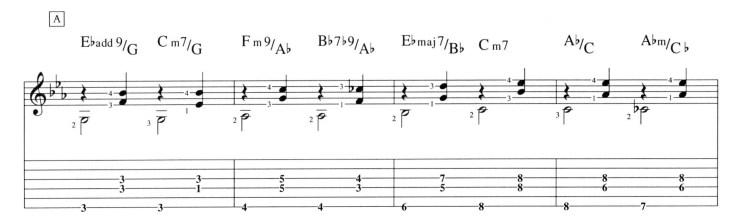

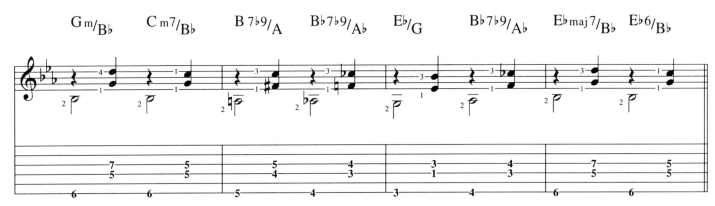

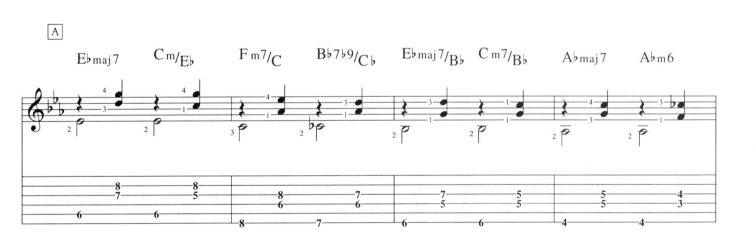

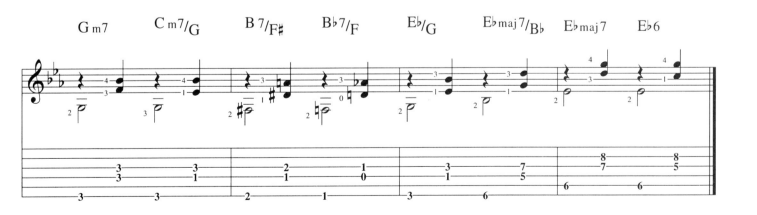

Can't Help Lovin' Dat Man

Arr. by Ron Berman

(Single-Note Solo)

Music by Jerome Kern
Words by Oscar Hammerstein II

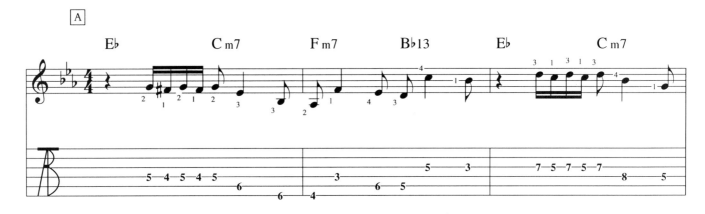

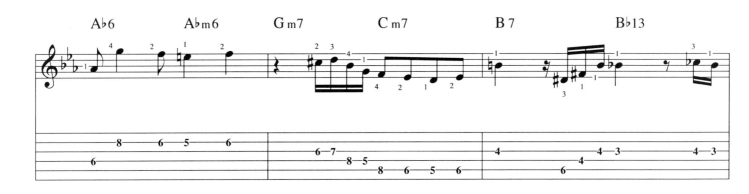

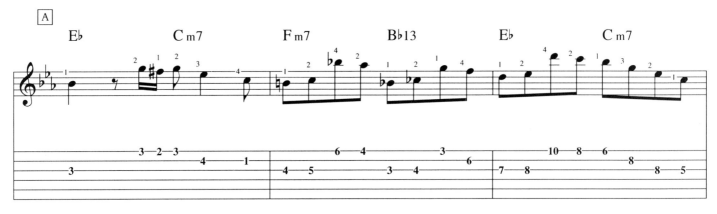

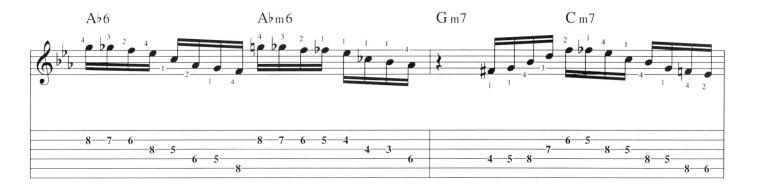

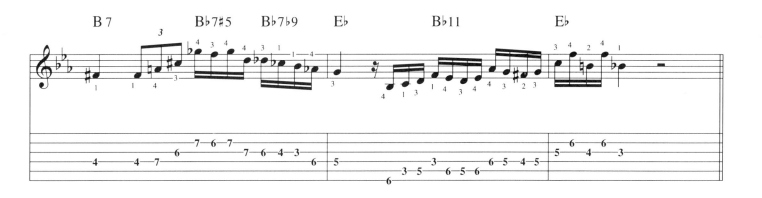

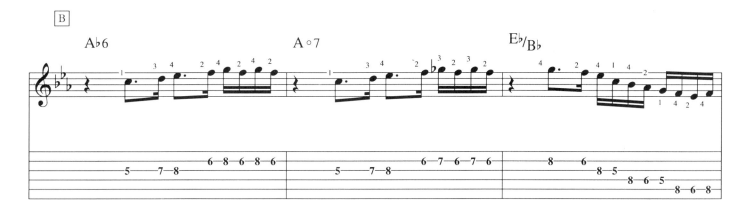

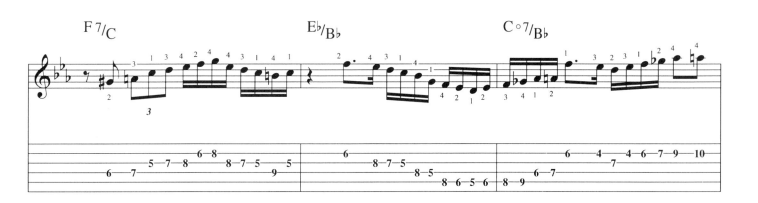

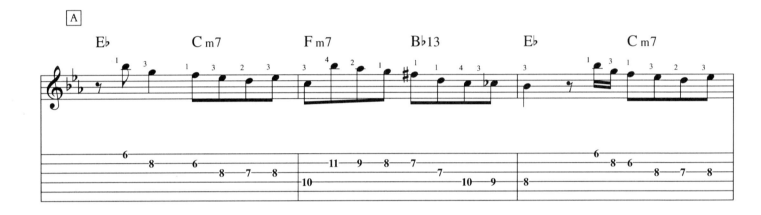

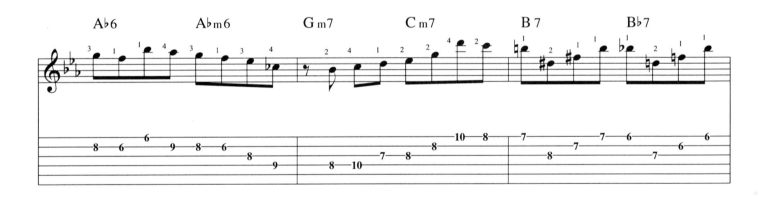

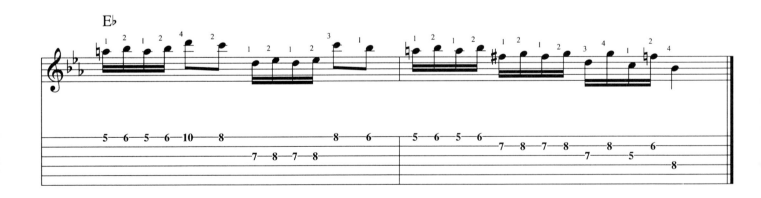

This page has been
left blank to avoid
awkward page turns.

EAST OF THE SUN
(AND WEST OF THE MOON)

Words and Music by
BROOKS BOWMAN

EAST OF THE SUN
(AND WEST OF THE MOON)
(CHORD MELODY)

Arr. by Chris Buzzelli

Words and Music by
Brooks Bowman

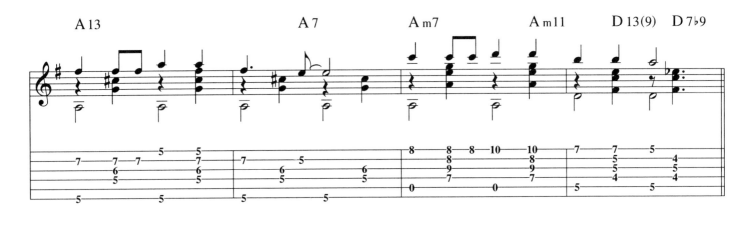

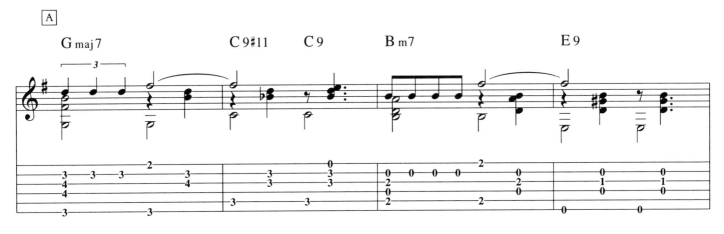

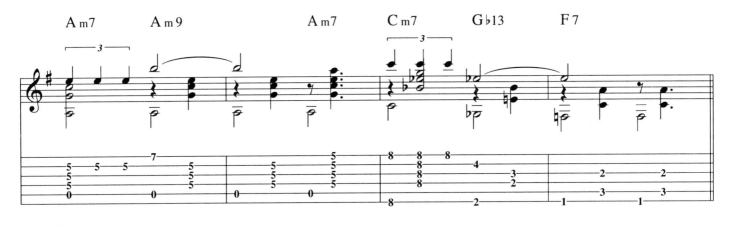

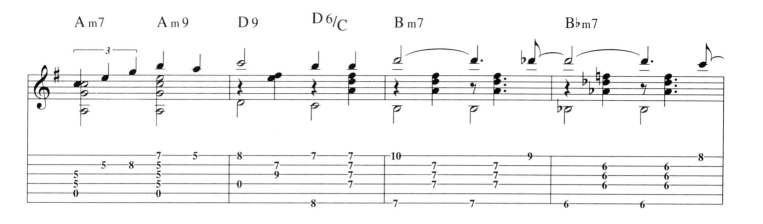

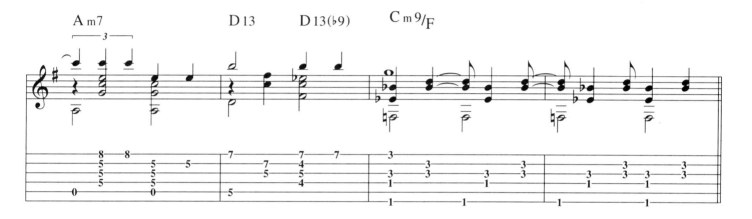

Outro

EAST OF THE SUN
(AND WEST OF THE MOON)
(COMPING ETUDE)

Arr. by CHRIS BUZZELLI

Words and Music by
BROOKS BOWMAN

EAST OF THE SUN
(AND WEST OF THE MOON)
(SINGLE-NOTE SOLO)

Arr. by CHRIS BUZZELLI

Words and Music by
BROOKS BOWMAN

Embraceable You

Music and Lyrics by
George Gershwin
and Ira Gershwin

B

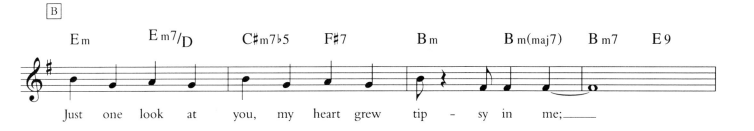

Just one look at you, my heart grew tip – sy in me;

you and you a – lone bring out the gyp – sy in me!

A

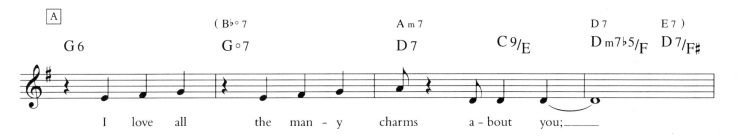

I love all the man – y charms a – bout you;

a – bove all I want my arms a – bout you.

C

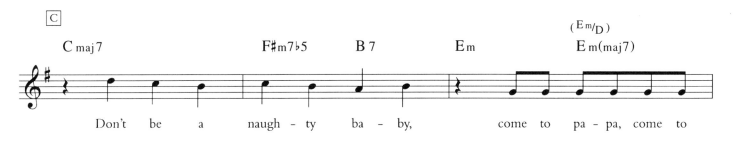

Don't be a naugh – ty ba – by, come to pa – pa, come to

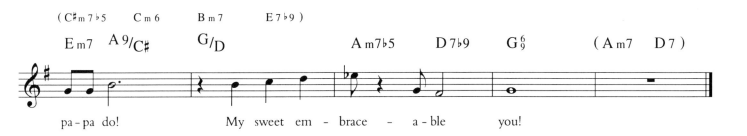

pa – pa do! My sweet em – brace – a – ble you!

EMBRACEABLE YOU

(CHORD MELODY)

Arr. by JACK WILKINS

Music and Lyrics by
GEORGE GERSHWIN
and IRA GERSHWIN

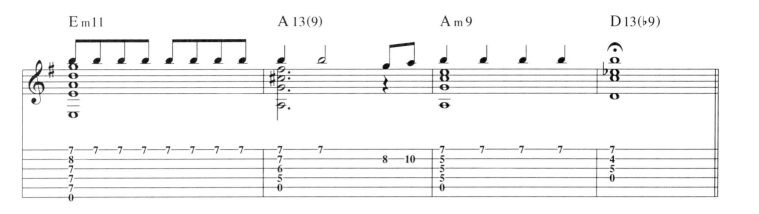

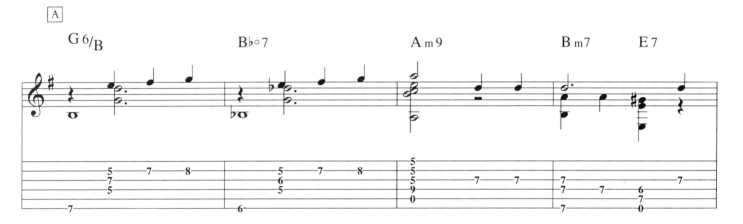

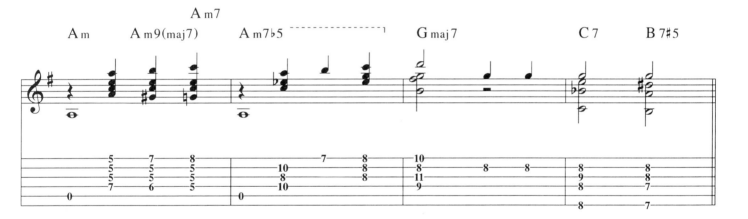

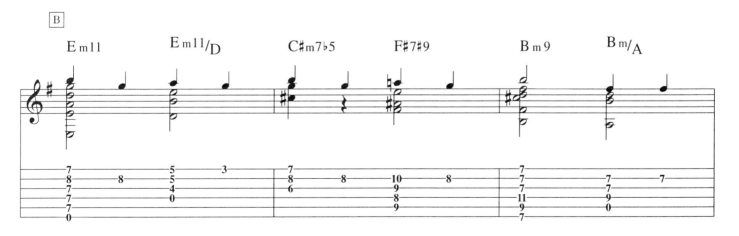

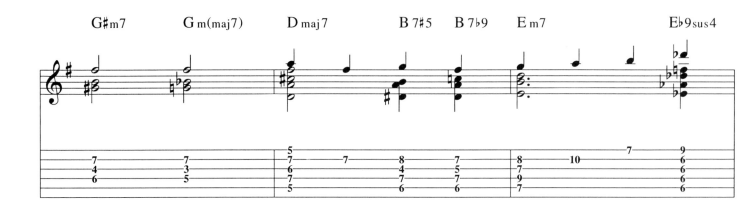

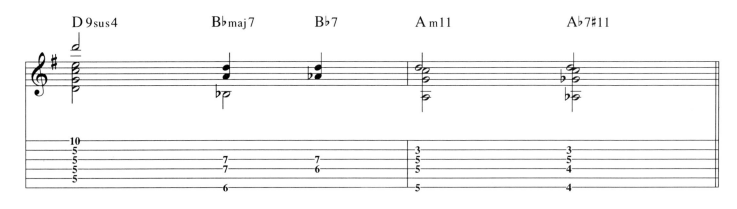

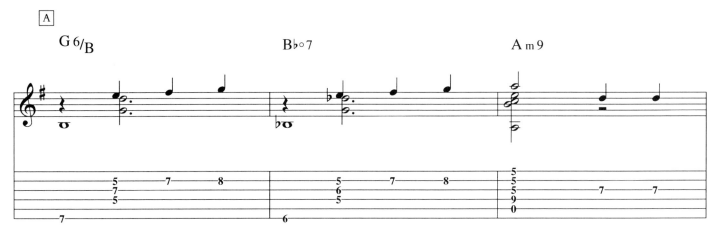

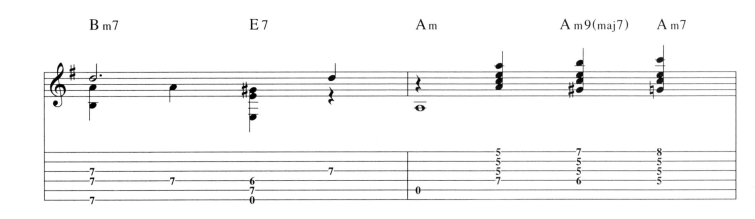

Embraceable You

(Comping Etude)

Arr. by Jack Wilkins

Music and Lyrics by
George Gershwin
and Ira Gershwin

Embraceable You
(Single-Note Solo)

Arr. by Jack Wilkins

Music and Lyrics by
George Gershwin
and Ira Gershwin

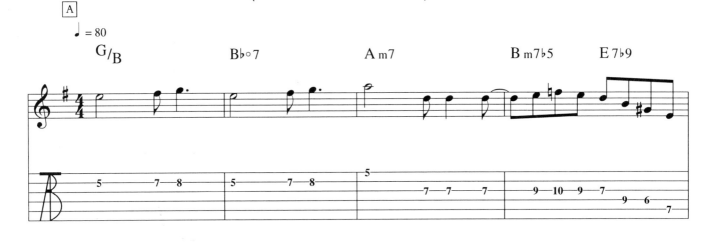

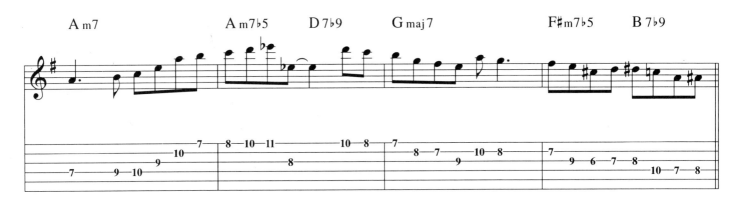

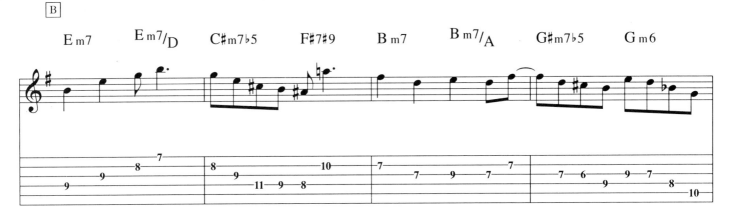

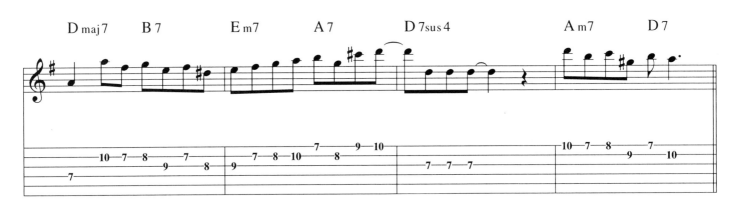

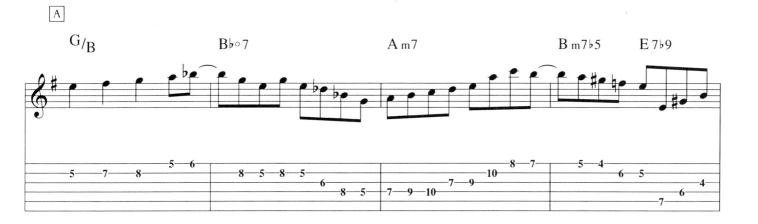

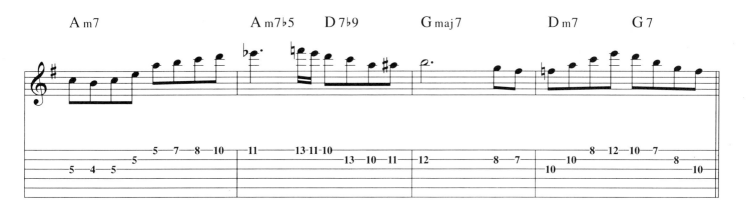

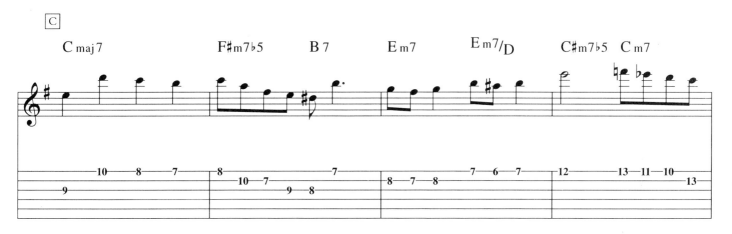

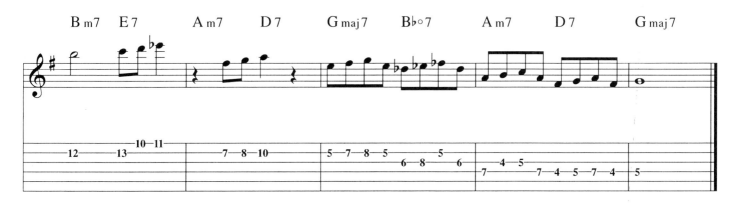

In Your Own Sweet Way

Words and Music by Dave Brubeck

In Your Own Sweet Way

Arr. by Chris Buzzelli

(Chord Melody)

Words and Music by Dave Brubeck

In Your Own Sweet Way

Arr. by Chris Buzzelli

(Comping Etude)

Words and Music by Dave Brubeck

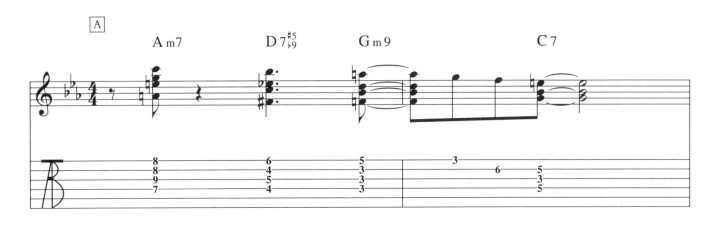

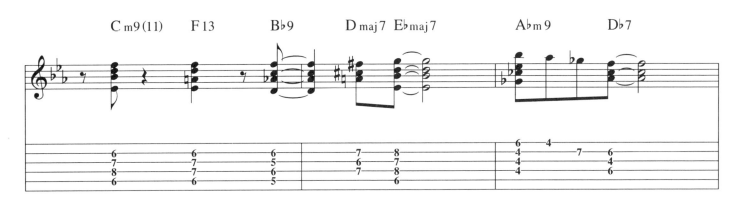

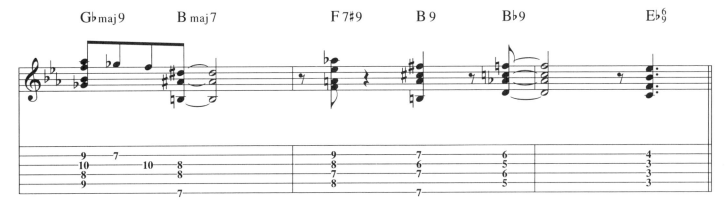

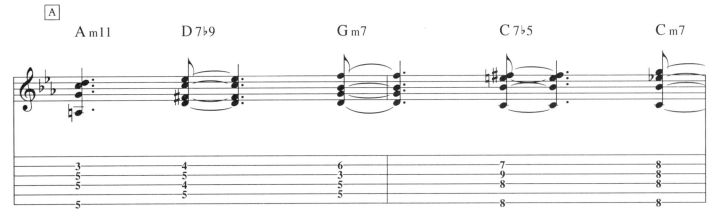

In Your Own Sweet Way

Arr. by Chris Buzzelli

(Single-Note Solo)

Words and Music by Dave Brubeck

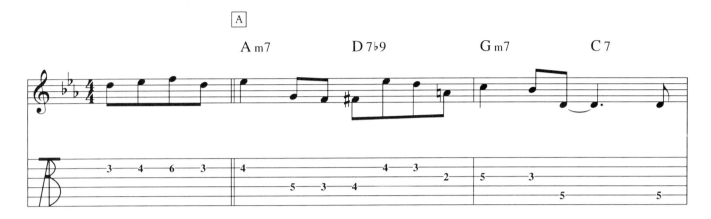

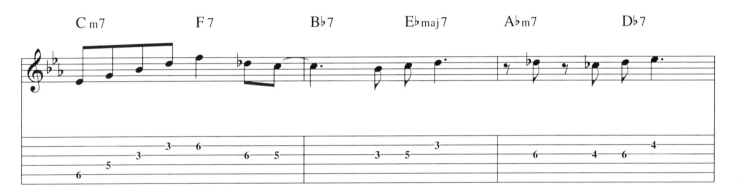

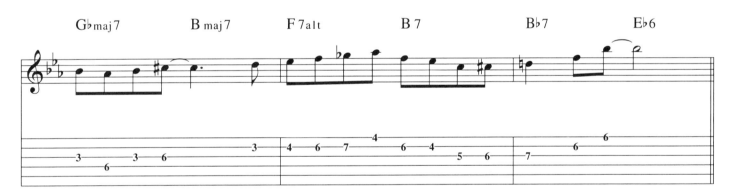

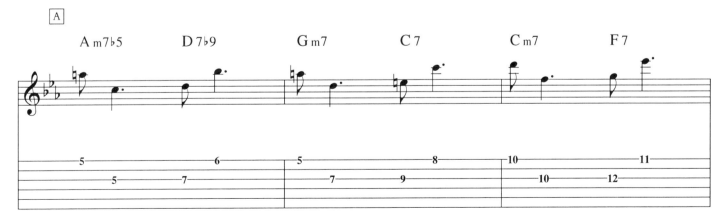

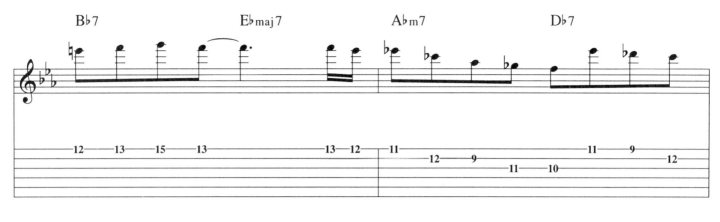

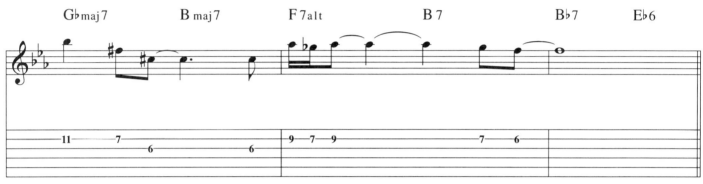

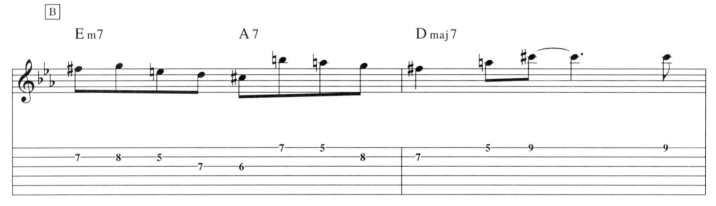

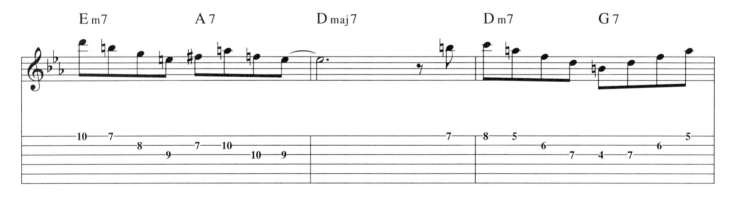

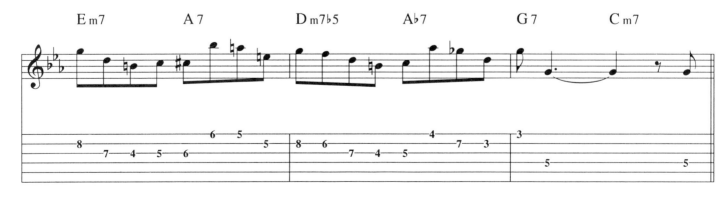

It Don't Mean a Thing
(If It Ain't Got That Swing)

Music by Duke Ellington
Words by Irving Mills

Verse
Rubato

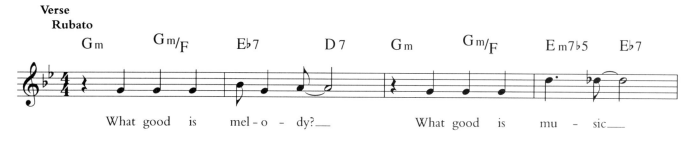

What good is mel-o-dy?___ What good is mu - sic___

if it ain't pos - sess-in' some - thing sweet?_____

It ain't the mel-o-dy.___ It ain't the mu - sic.___

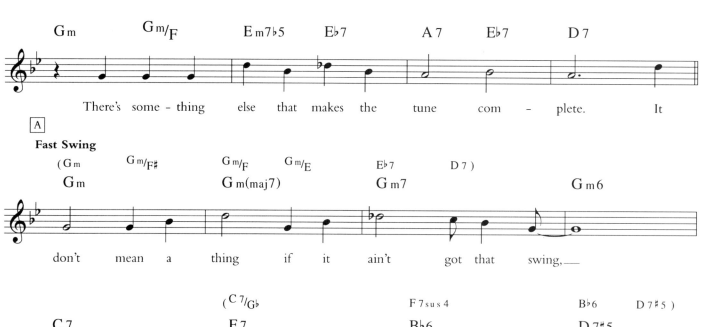

There's some - thing else that makes the tune com - plete. It

A

Fast Swing

don't mean a thing if it ain't got that swing,___

doo wah,___ doo wah, doo wah, doo wah, doo wah,___ doo wah, doo wah, doo wah. It

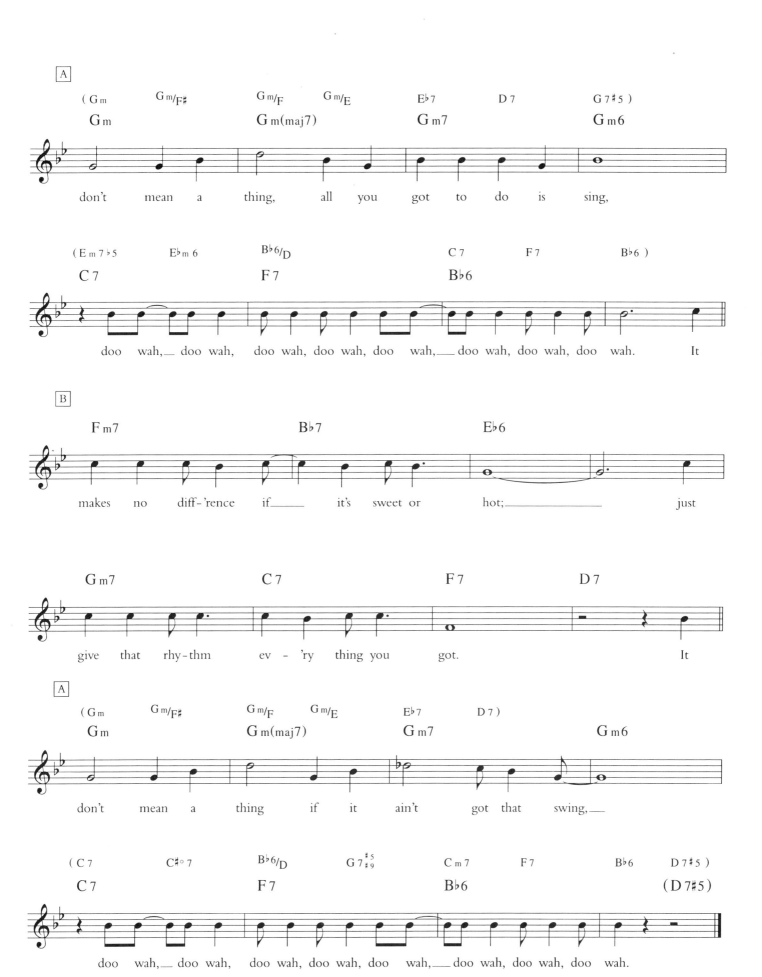

It Don't Mean a Thing
(If It Ain't Got That Swing)
(Chord Melody)

Arr. by Dave Frackenpohl

Music by Duke Ellington
Words by Irving Mills

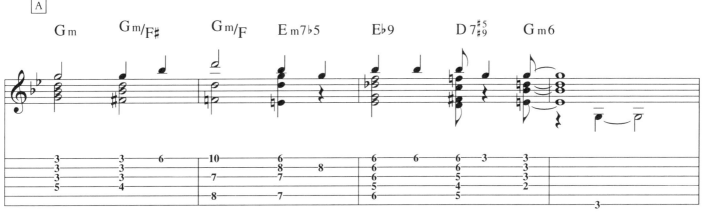

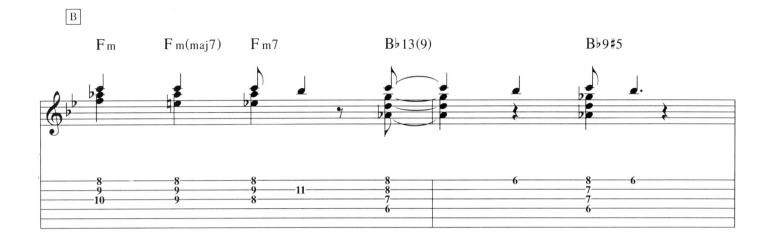

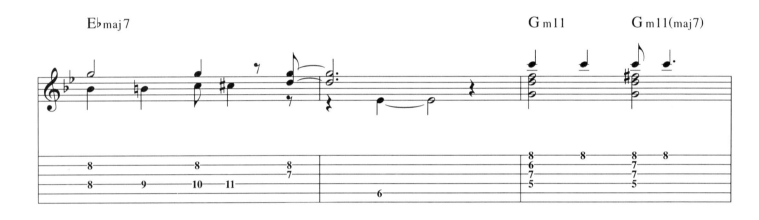

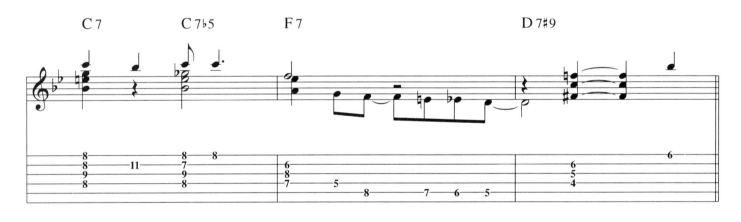

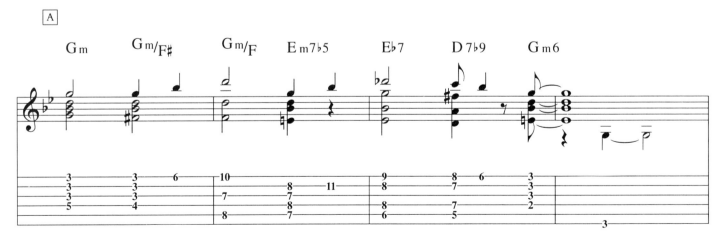

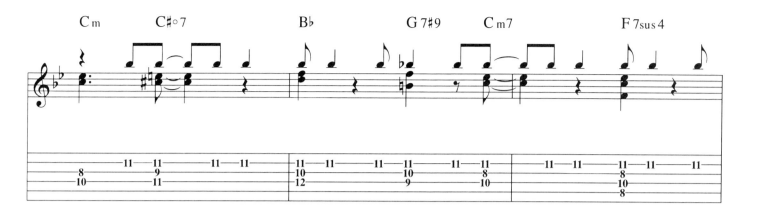

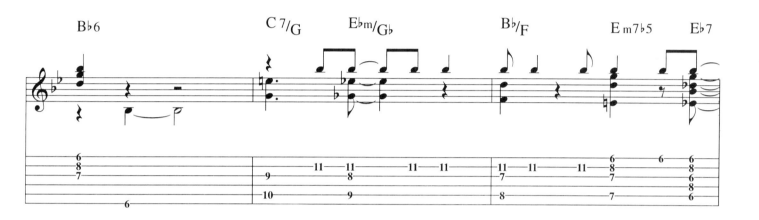

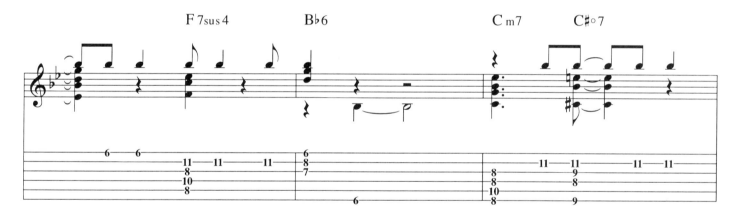

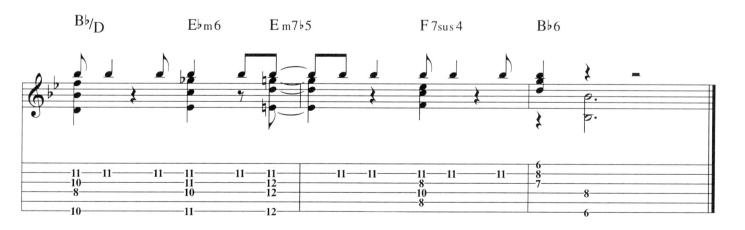

It Don't Mean a Thing
(If It Ain't Got That Swing)

(Comping Etude)

Arr. by Dave Frackenpohl

Music by Duke Ellington
Words by Irving Mills

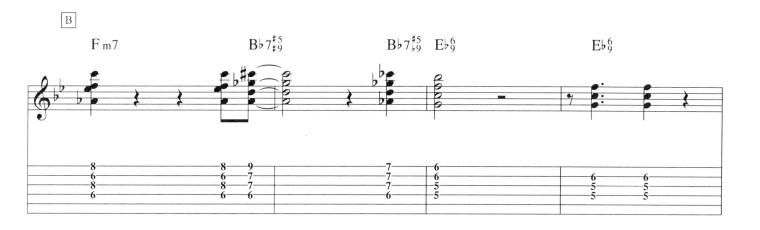

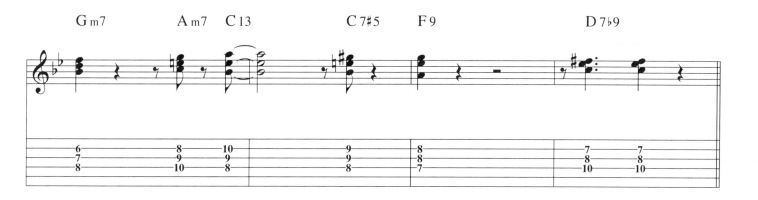

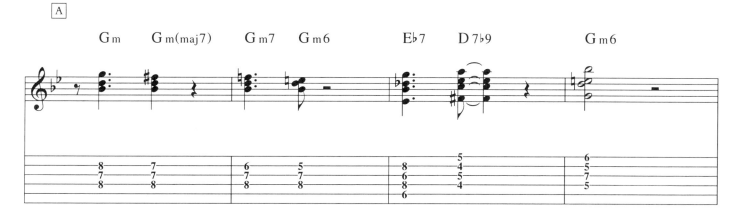

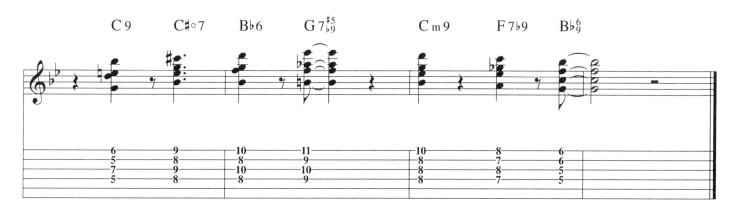

It Don't Mean a Thing
(If It Ain't Got That Swing)
(Single-Note Solo)

Arr. by Dave Frackenpohl

Music by Duke Ellington
Words by Irving Mills

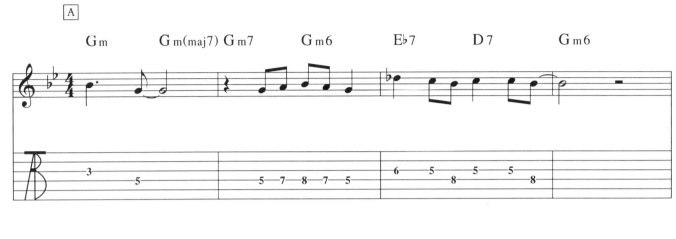

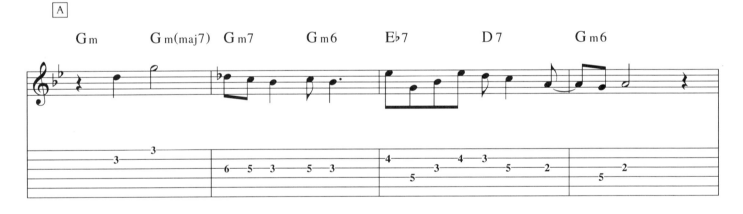

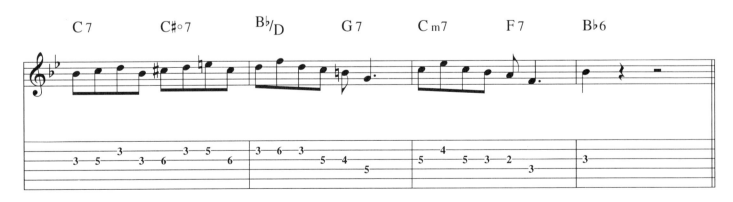

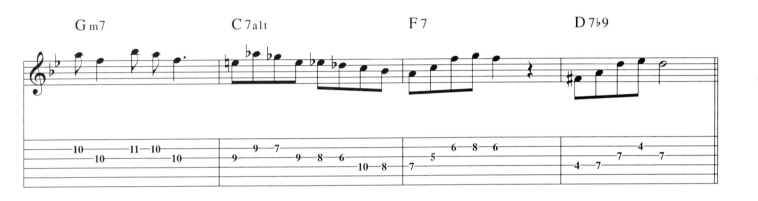

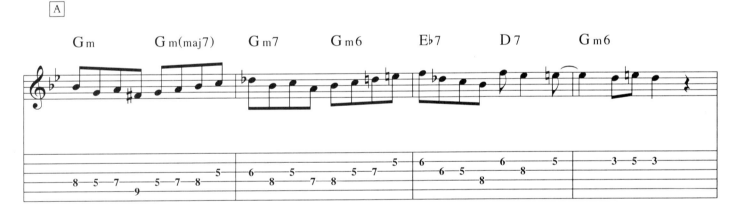

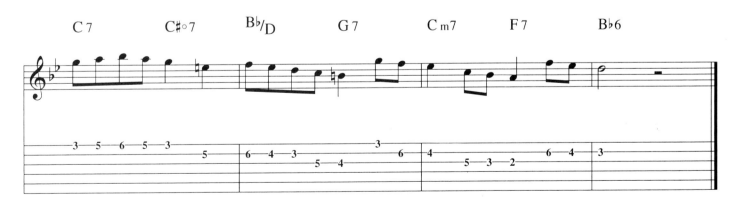

I've Got You Under My Skin

Words and Music by Cole Porter

I've Got You Under My Skin

Arr. by Ron Berman

(CHORD MELODY)

Words and Music by Cole Porter

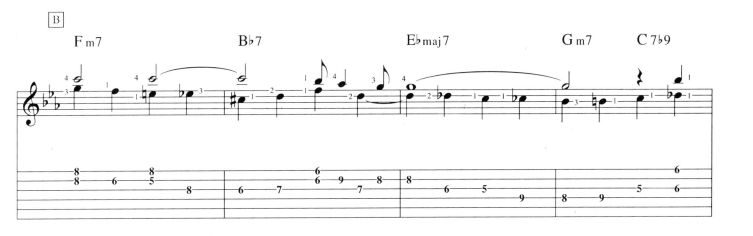

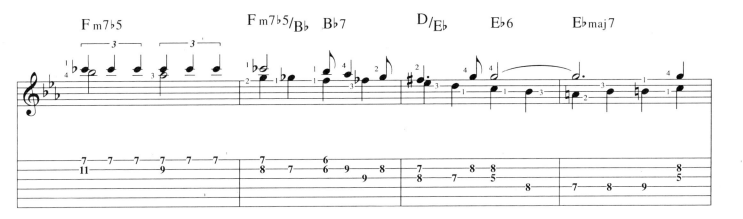

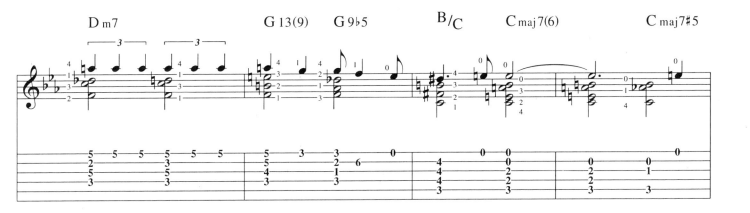

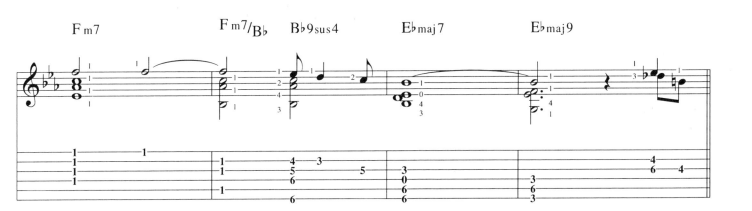

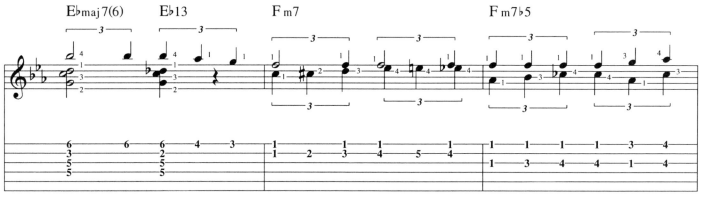

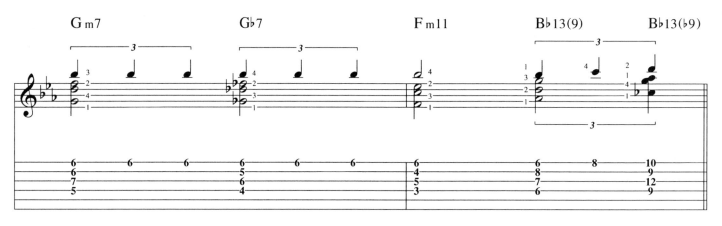

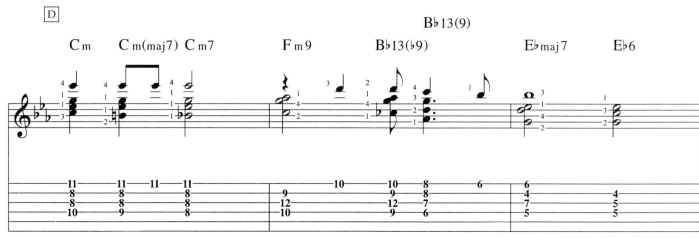

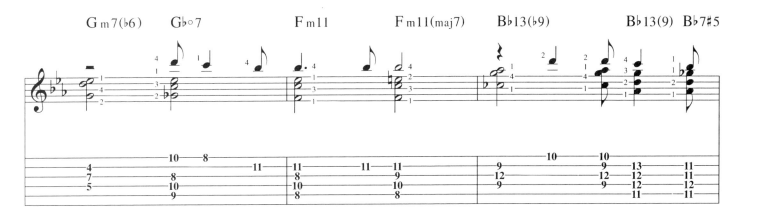

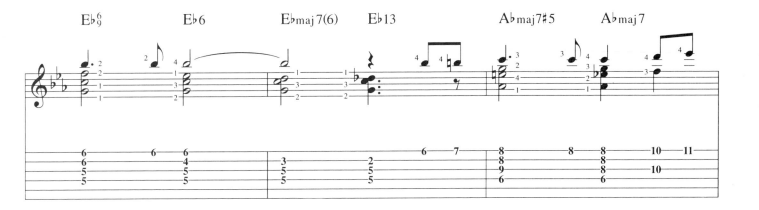

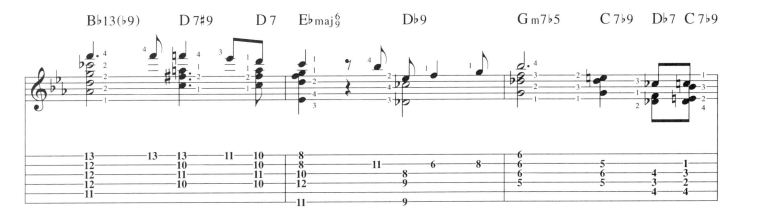

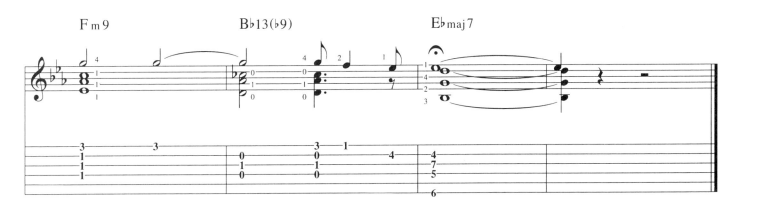

I've Got You Under My Skin

Arr. by Ron Berman

(Comping Etude)

Words and Music by Cole Porter

I've Got You Under My Skin

Arr. by Ron Berman

(SINGLE-NOTE SOLO)

Words and Music by Cole Porter

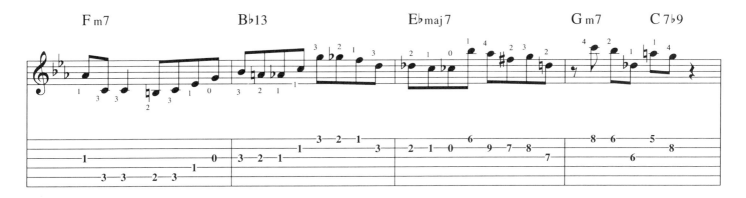

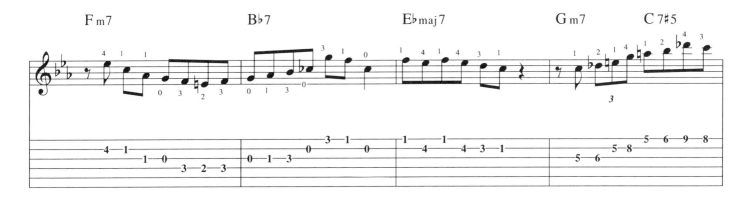

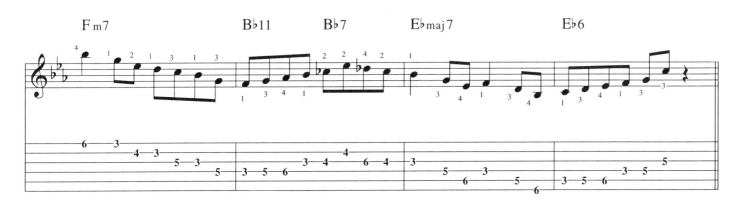

Long Ago
(and Far Away)

Lyrics by IRA GERSHWIN
Music by JEROME KERN

A

Moderately Slow

Long a-go and far a-way, I dreamed a dream one
day and now that dream is here be-side me.

B

Long the skies were o-ver-cast, but now the clouds have
passed: you're here at last!___

A

Chills run up and down my spine, A-lad-din's lamp is
mine, the dream I dreamed was not de-nied me.

C

Just one look and then I knew___ that all I
longed for, long a-go was you.___

LONG AGO
(AND FAR AWAY)
(CHORD MELODY)

Arr. by Jack Wilkins

Lyrics by Ira Gershwin
Music by Jerome Kern

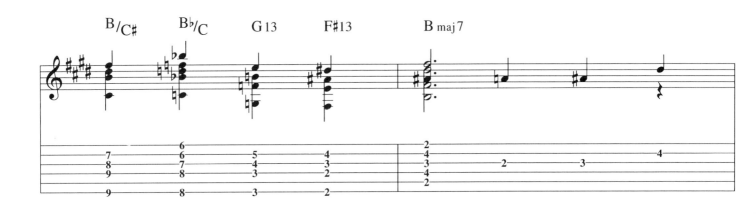

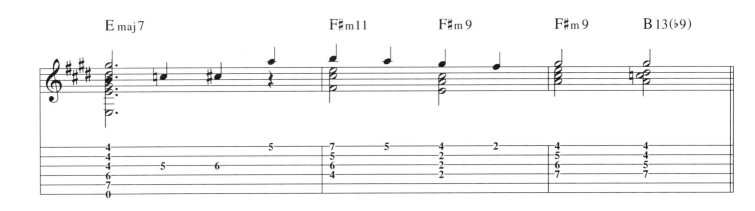

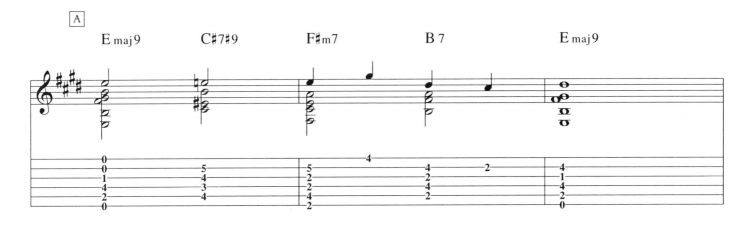

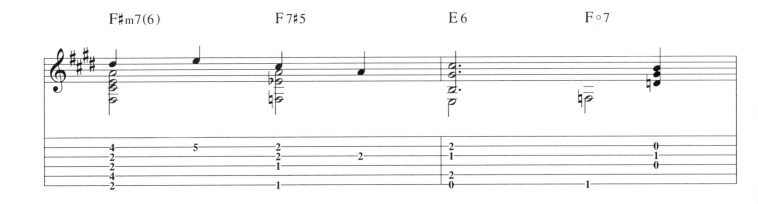

Long Ago
(and Far Away)
(Comping Etude)

Arr. by Jack Wilkins

Lyrics by Ira Gershwin
Music by Jerome Kern

115

LONG AGO
(AND FAR AWAY)
(SINGLE-NOTE SOLO)

Arr. by JACK WILKINS

Lyrics by IRA GERSHWIN
Music by JEROME KERN

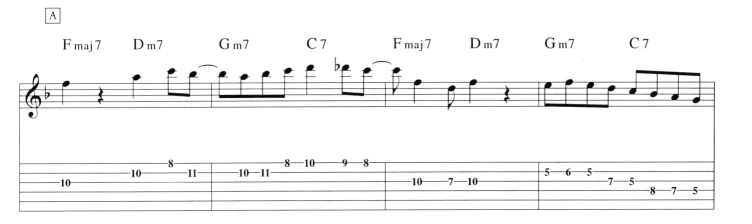

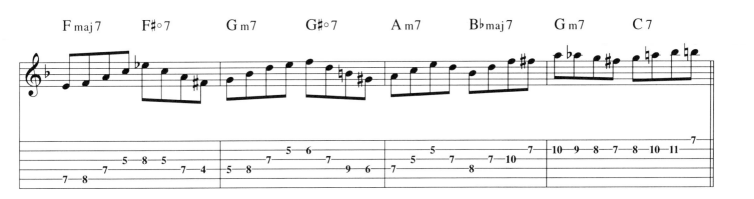

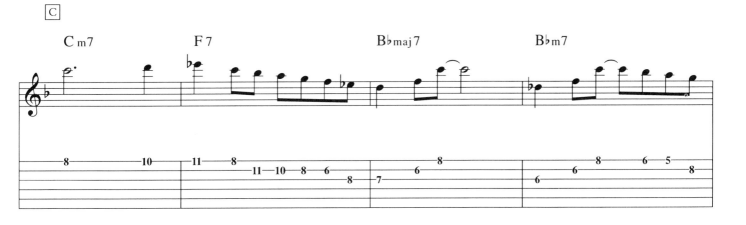

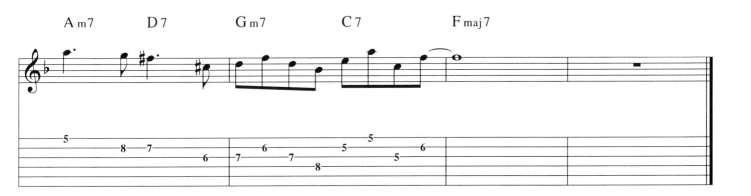

Misty

Words by Johnny Burke
Music by Erroll Garner

Misty
(Chord Melody)

Arr. by Rick Stone

Words by Johnny Burke
Music by Erroll Garner

MISTY
(COMPING ETUDE)

Arr. by RICK STONE

Words by JOHNNY BURKE
Music by ERROLL GARNER

123

Misty
(Single-Note Solo)

Arr. by Rick Stone

Words by Johnny Burke
Music by Erroll Garner

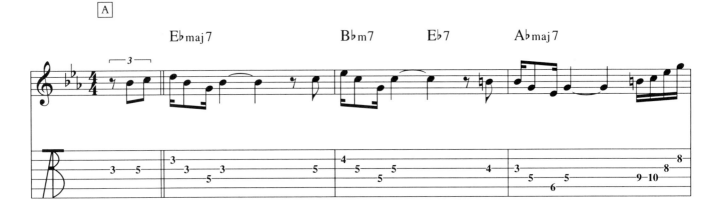

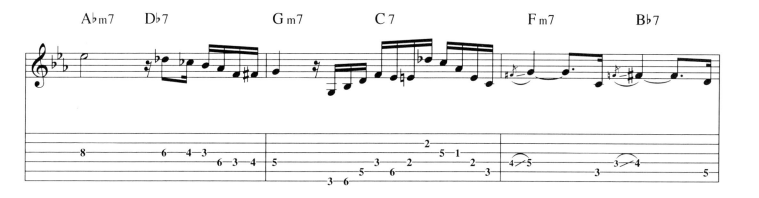

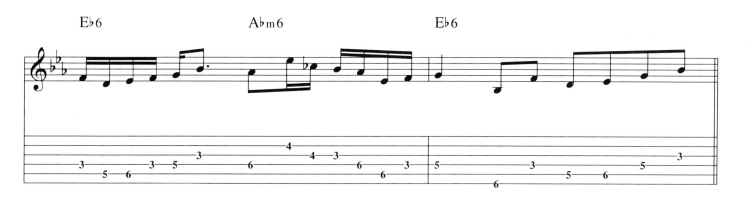

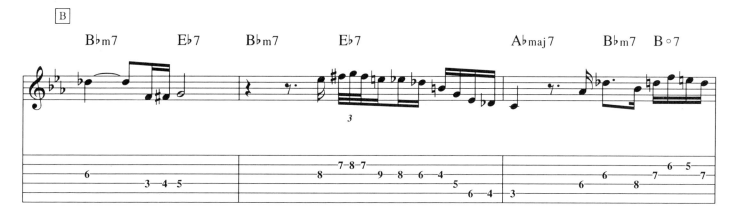

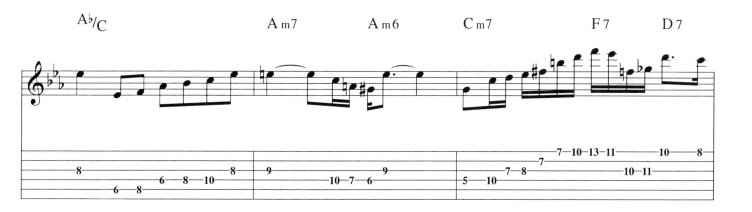

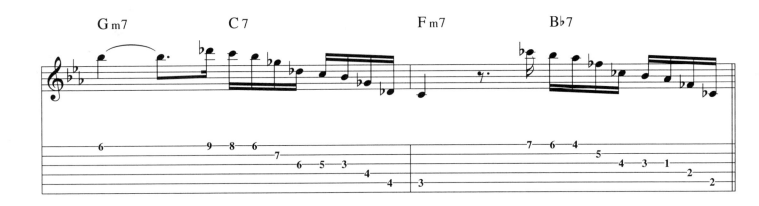

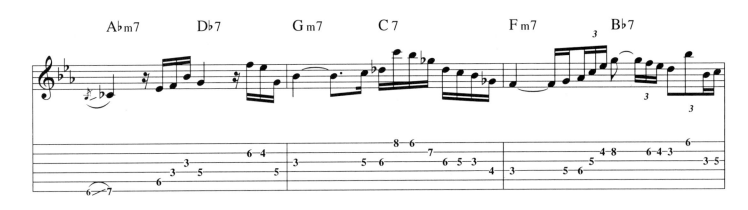

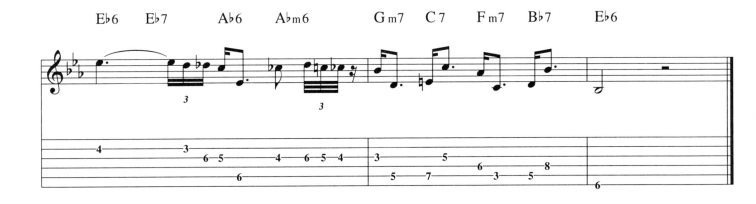

My Funny Valentine

Words by Lorenz Hart
Music by Richard Rodgers

127

MY FUNNY VALENTINE

(CHORD MELODY)

Arr. by LaRue Nickelson

Words by Lorenz Hart
Music by Richard Rodgers

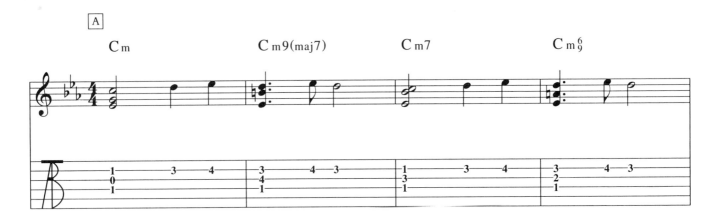

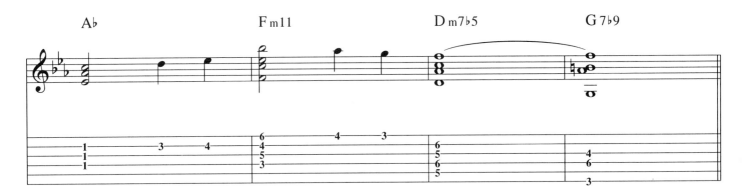

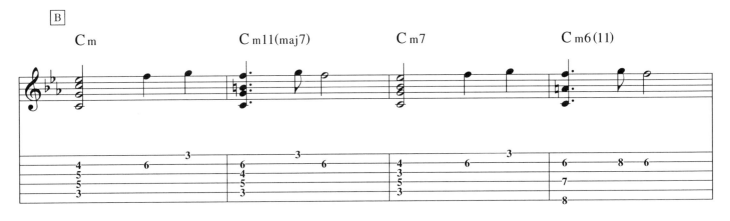

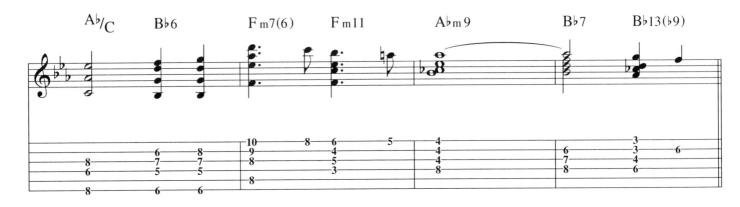

MY FUNNY VALENTINE

Arr. by LaRue Nickelson

(COMPING ETUDE)

Words by Lorenz Hart
Music by Richard Rodgers

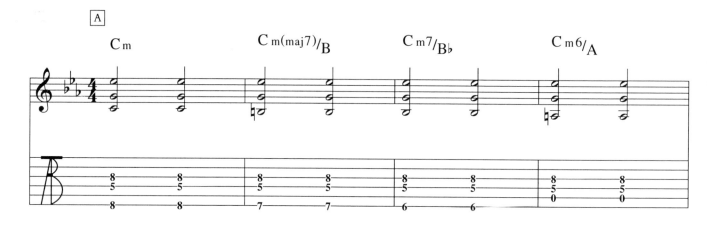

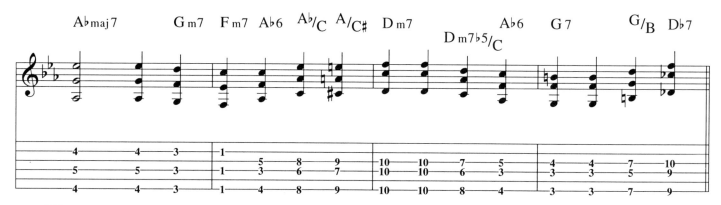

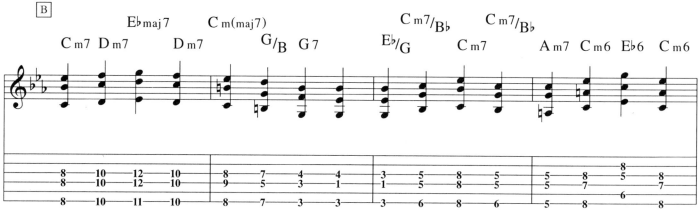

MY FUNNY VALENTINE

(SINGLE-NOTE SOLO)

Arr. by LaRue Nickelson

Words by Lorenz Hart
Music by Richard Rodgers

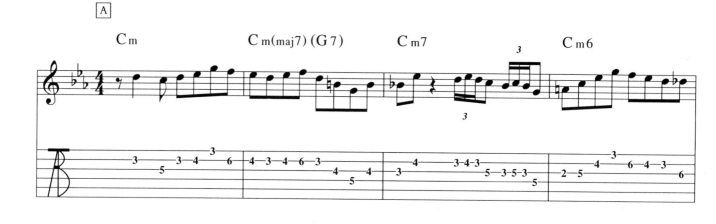

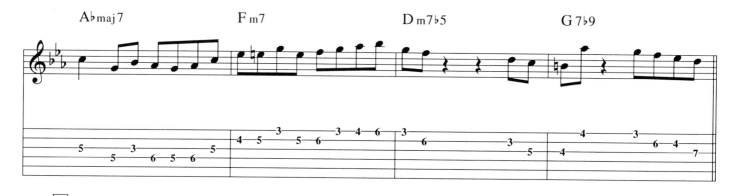

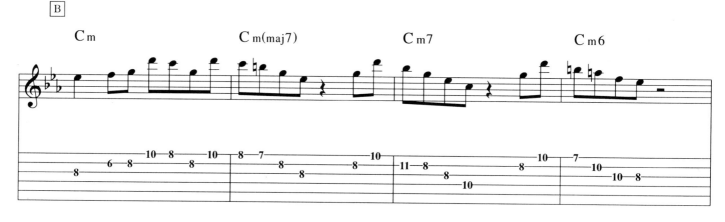

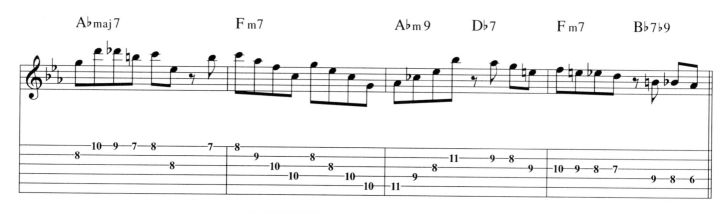

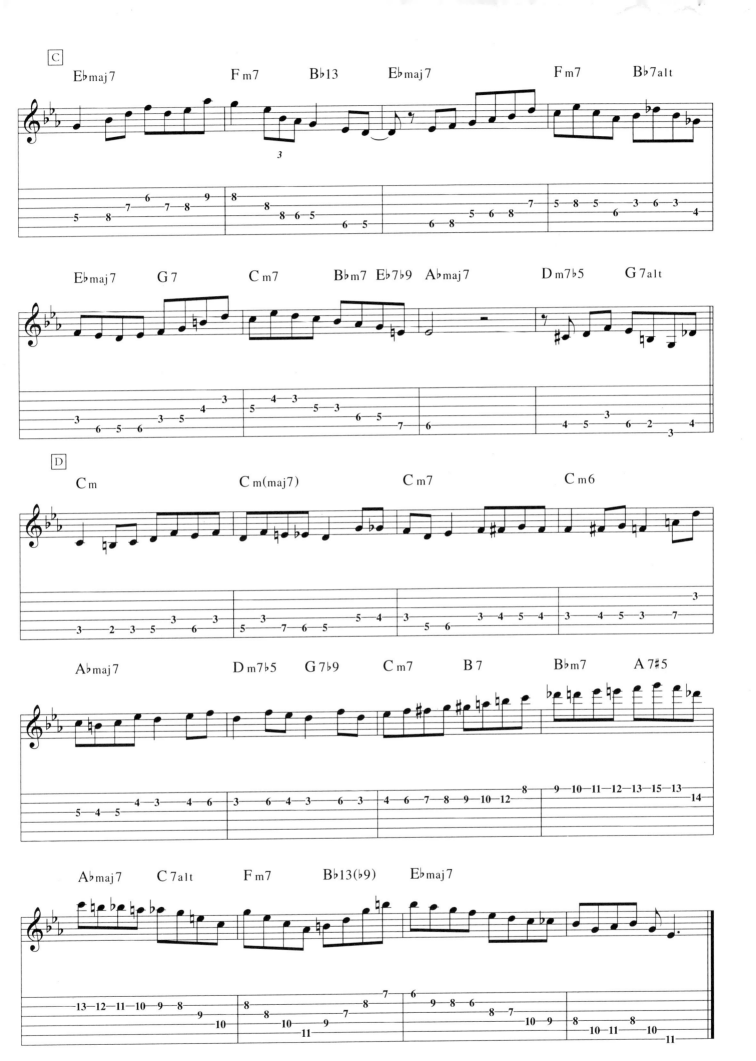

Night and Day

Music and Lyrics by
Cole Porter

NIGHT AND DAY

(CHORD MELODY)

Arr. by LaRue Nickelson

Music and Lyrics by
Cole Porter

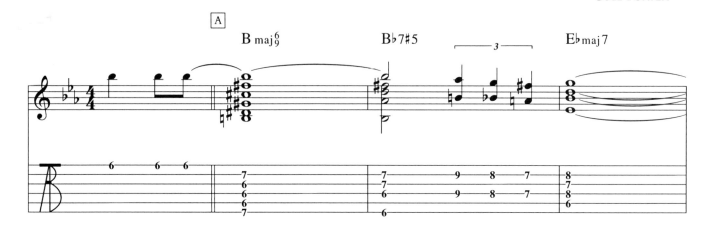

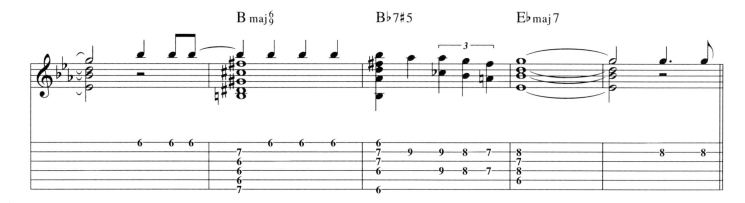

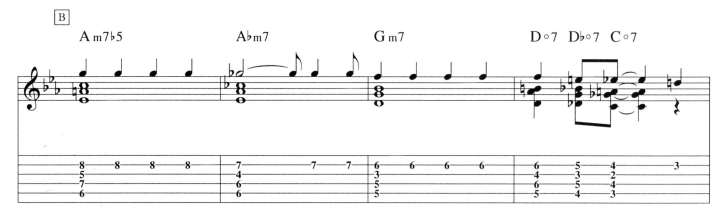

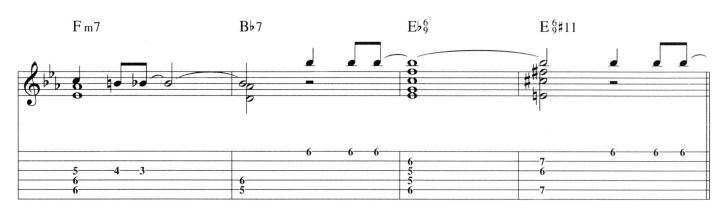

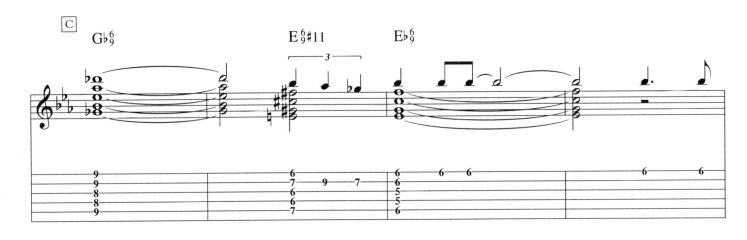

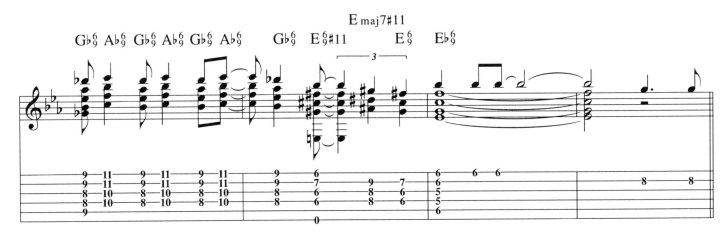

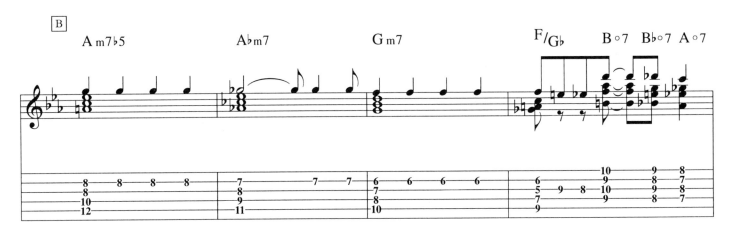

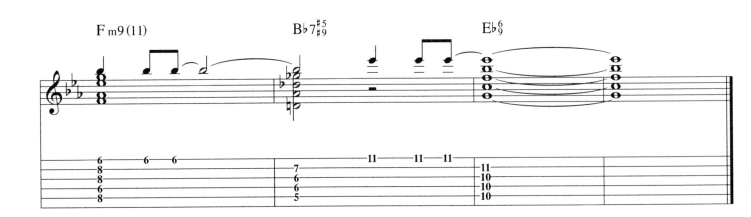

Night and Day
(Comping Etude)

Arr. by LaRue Nickelson

Music and Lyrics by
Cole Porter

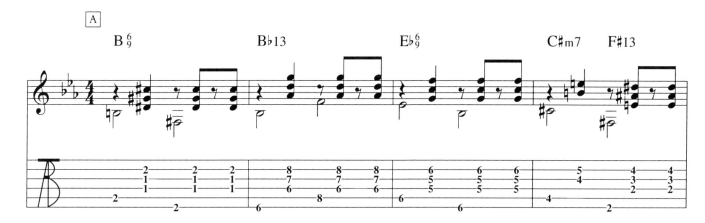

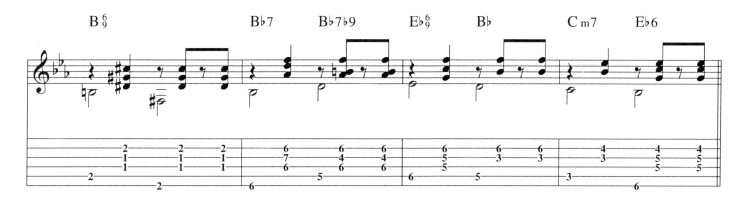

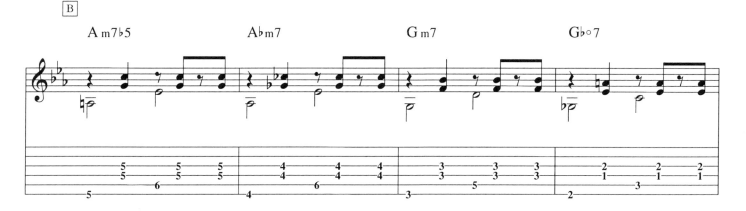

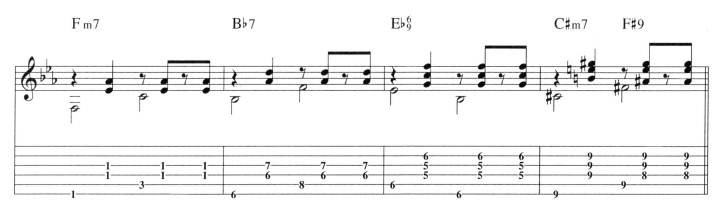

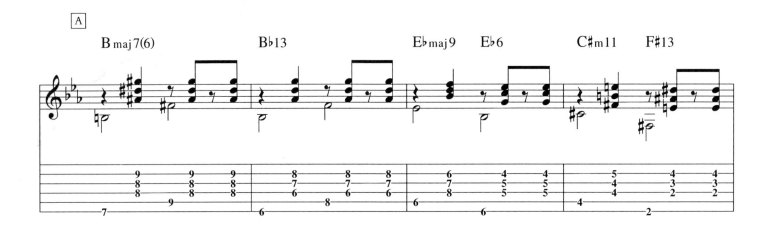

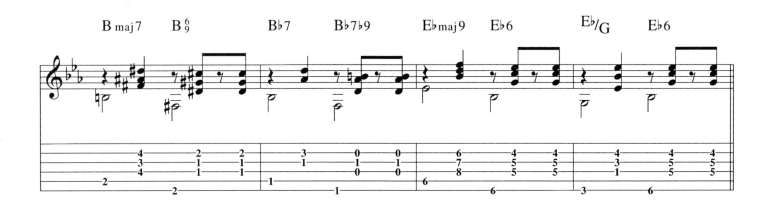

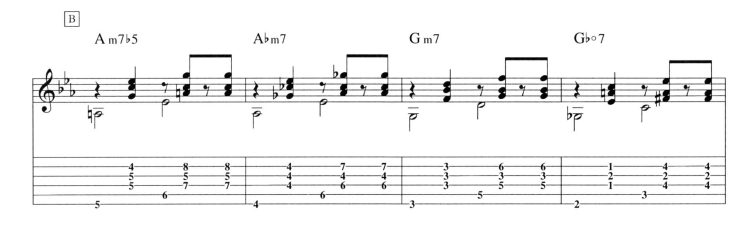

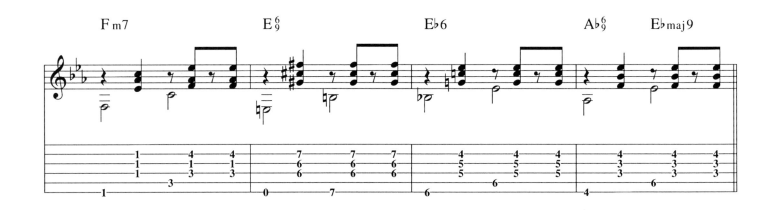

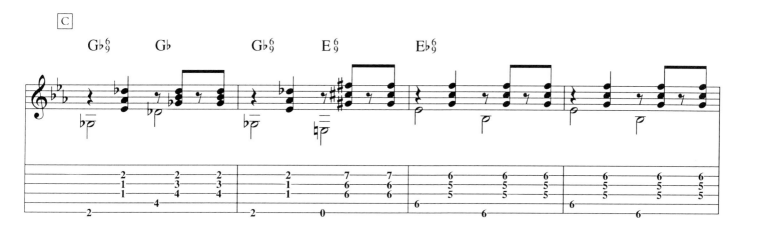

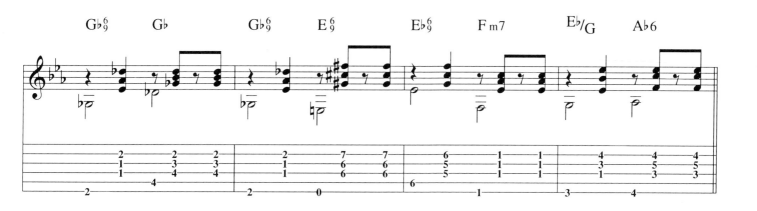

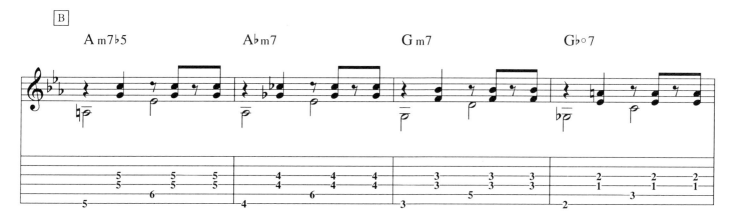

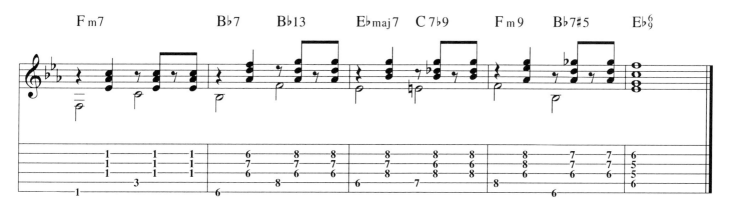

NIGHT AND DAY
(SINGLE-NOTE SOLO)

Arr. by LaRue Nickelson

Music and Lyrics by
COLE PORTER

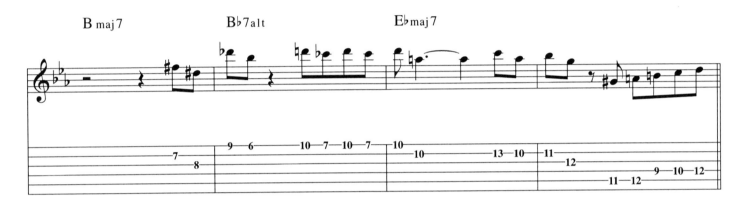

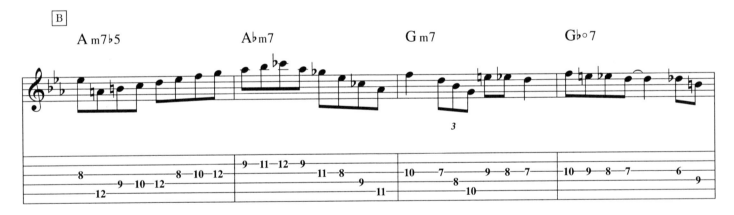

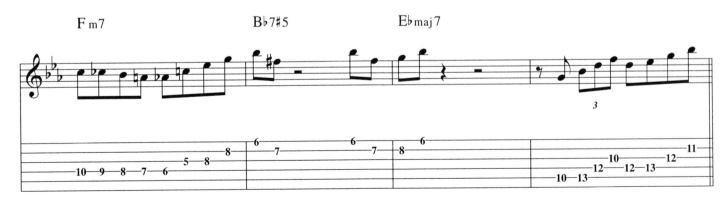

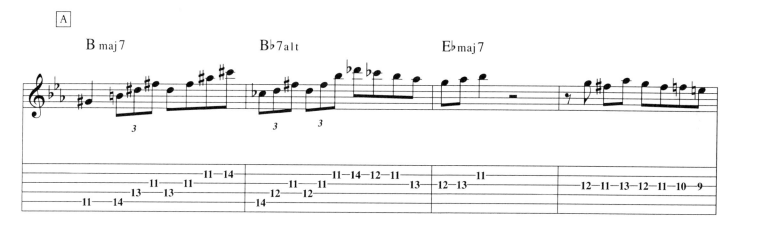

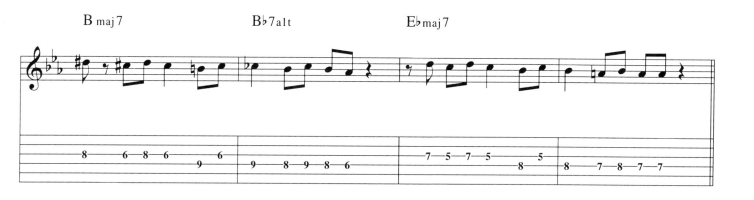

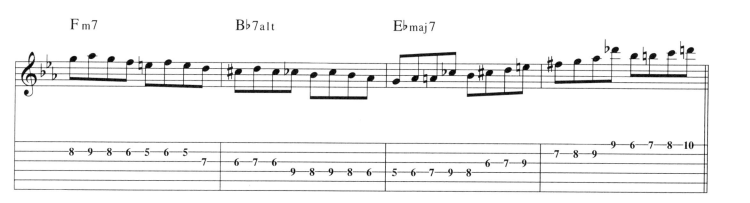

143

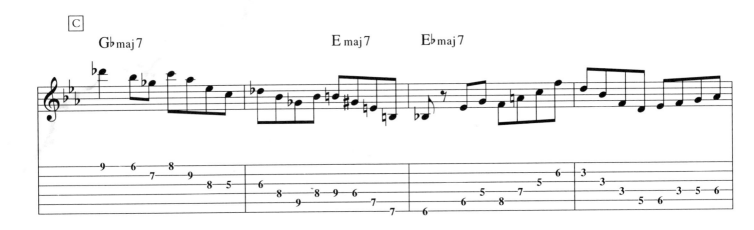

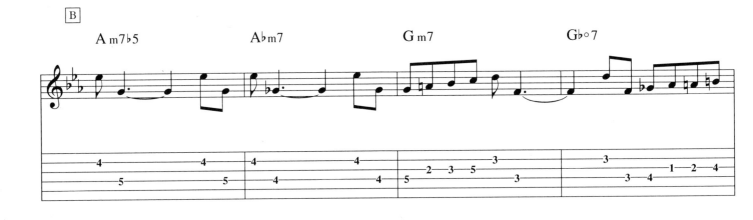

144

Smoke Gets In Your Eyes

Music by Jerome Kern
Words by Otto Harbach

Smoke Gets In Your Eyes

(Chord Melody)

Arr. by Sid Jacobs

Music by Jerome Kern
Words by Otto Harbach

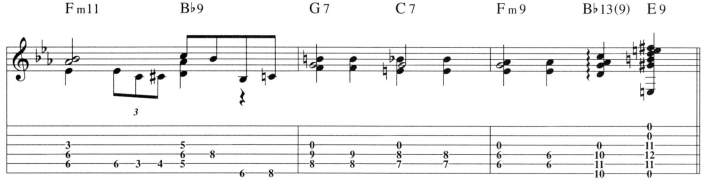

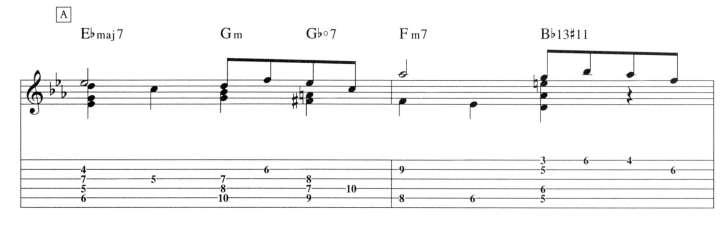

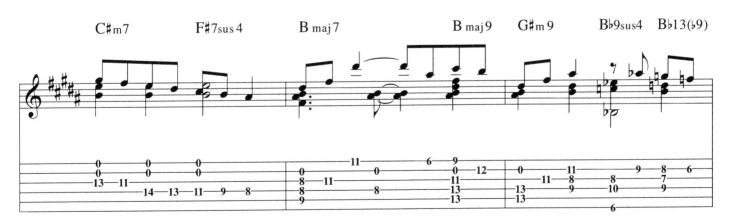

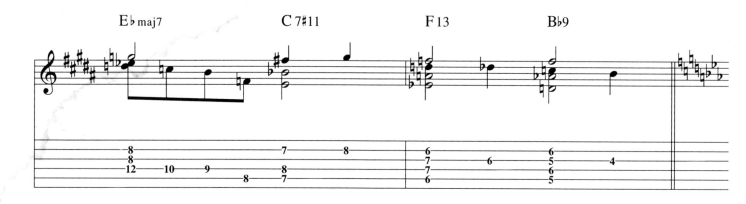

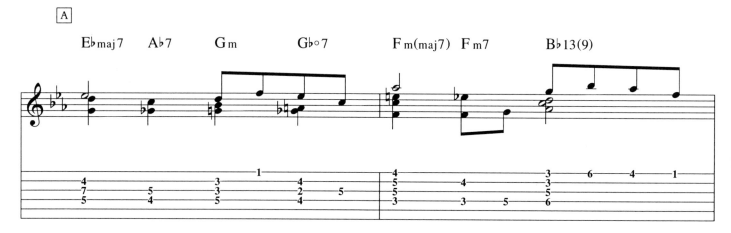

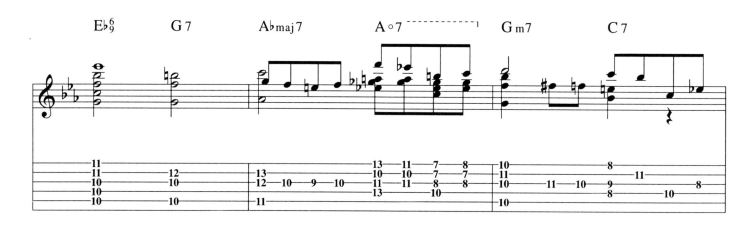

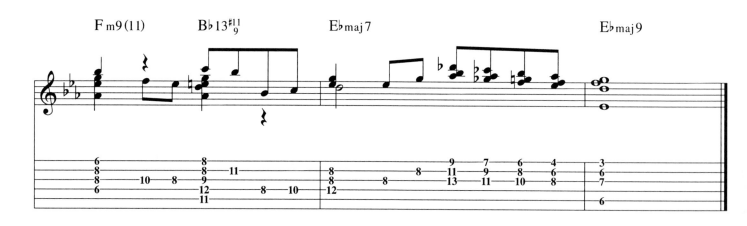

This page has been left blank to avoid awkward page turns.

SMOKE GETS IN YOUR EYES

(COMPING ETUDE)

Arr. by SID JACOBS

Music by JEROME KERN
Words by OTTO HARBACH

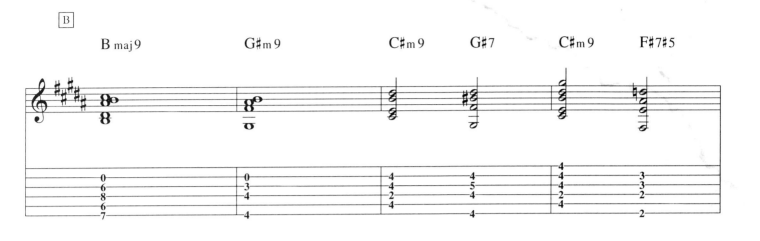

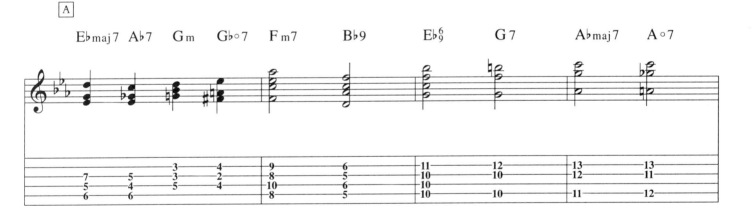

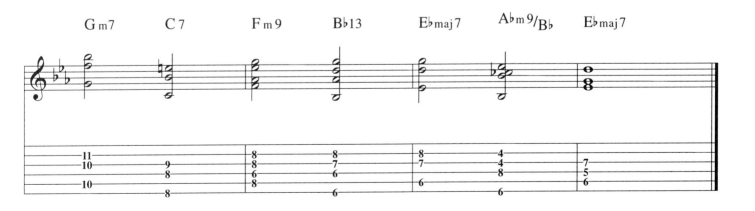

Smoke Gets In Your Eyes

(Single-Note Solo)

Arr. by Sid Jacobs

Music by Jerome Kern
Words by Otto Harbach

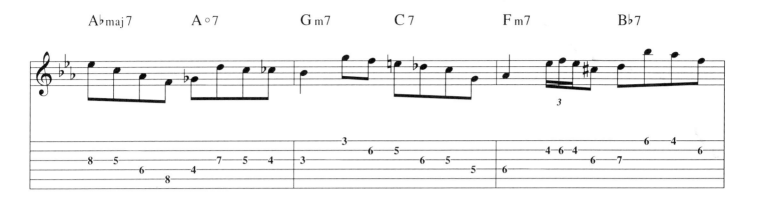

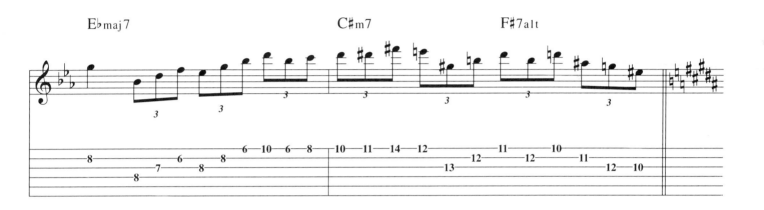

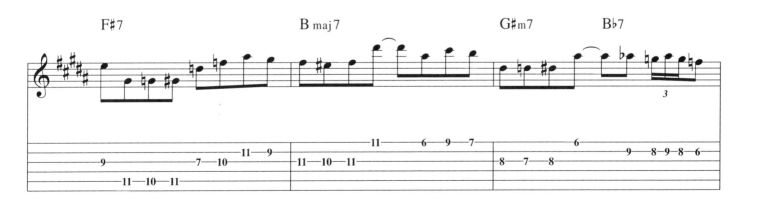

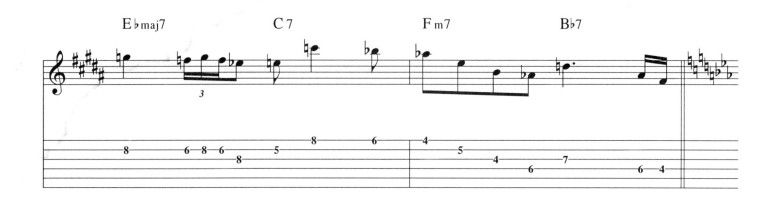

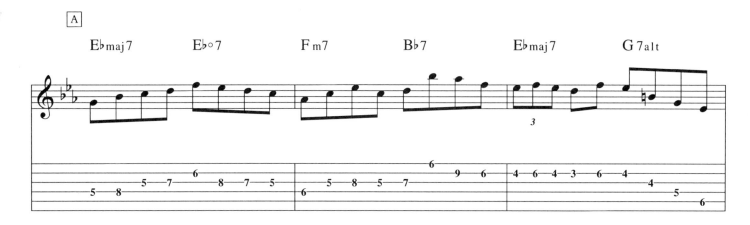

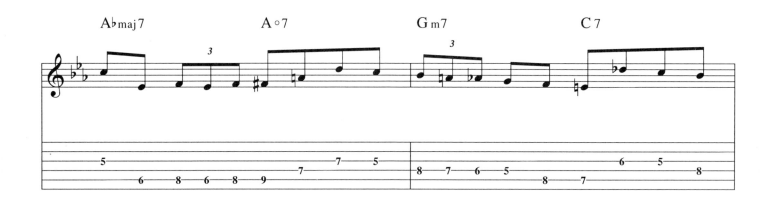

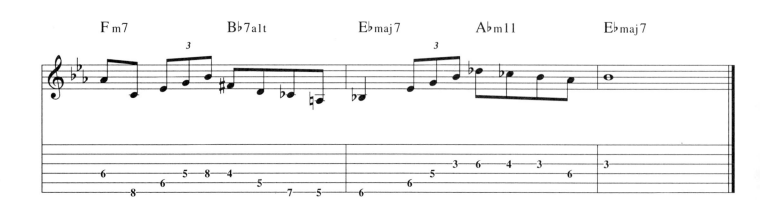

This page has been left blank to avoid awkward page turns.

Someone To Watch Over Me

Music and Lyrics by
George Gershwin
and Ira Gershwin

Verse
Moderately

There's a say-ing old says that love is blind. Still we're of-ten told, "Seek and ye shall find."

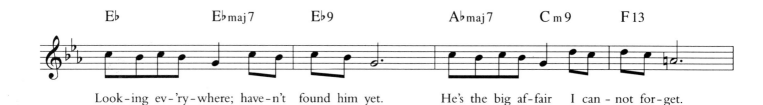

So, I'm going to seek a cer-tain lad I've had in mind.

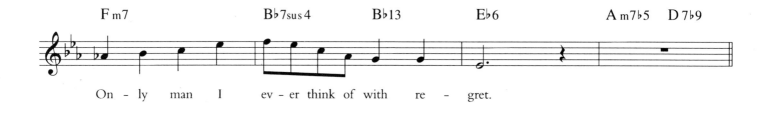

Look-ing ev-'ry-where; have-n't found him yet. He's the big af-fair I can-not for-get.

On - ly man I ev - er think of with re - gret.

I'd like to add his in - i - tial to my mon - o - gram.

Tell me, where is the shep-herd for this lost lamb?

156

SOMEONE TO WATCH OVER ME

Arr. by JACK WILKINS

(CHORD MELODY)

Music and Lyrics by
GEORGE GERSHWIN
and IRA GERSHWIN

159

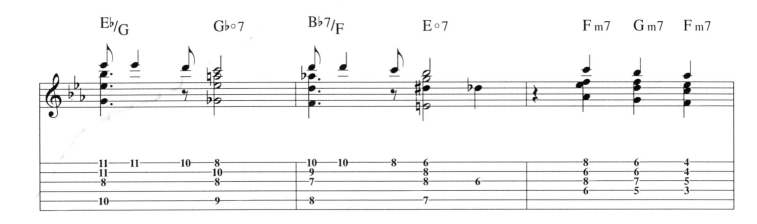

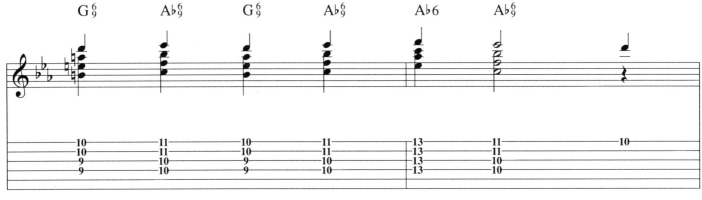

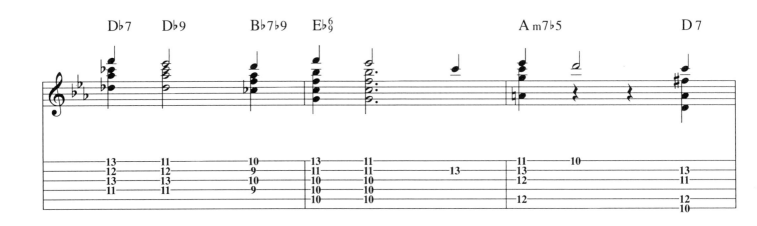

Someone To Watch Over Me

Arr. by Jack Wilkins

(Comping Etude)

Music and Lyrics by
George Gershwin
and Ira Gershwin

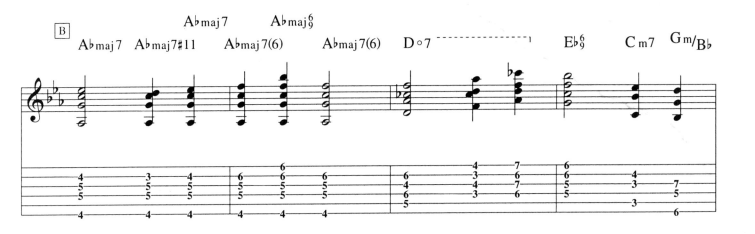

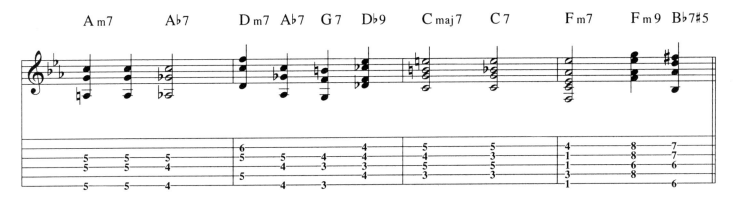

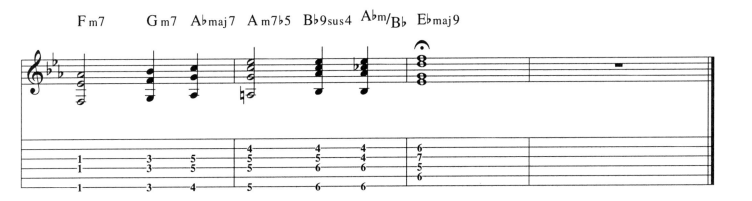

Someone To Watch Over Me

Arr. by Jack Wilkins

(Single-Note Solo)

Music and Lyrics by
George Gershwin
and Ira Gershwin

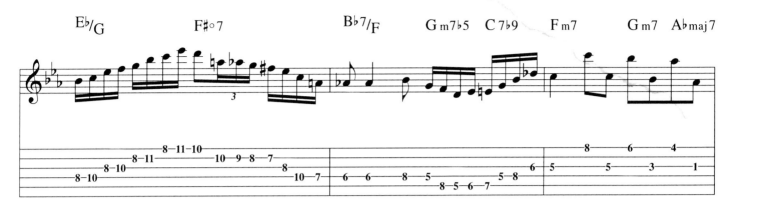

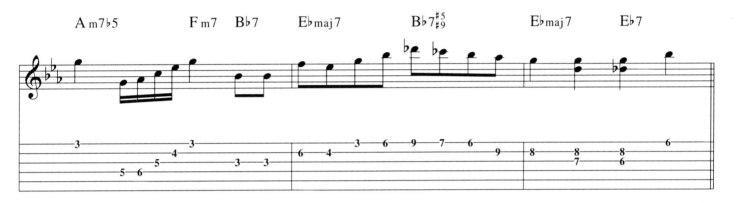

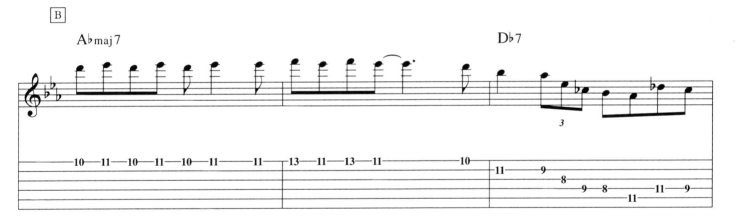

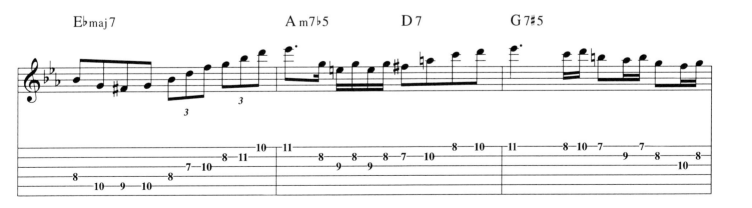

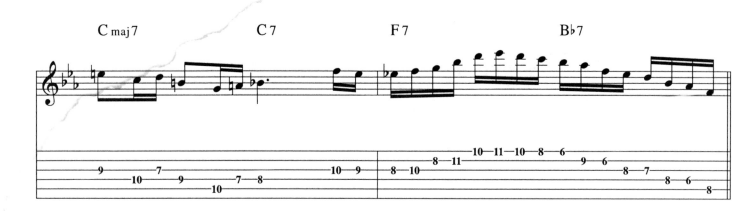

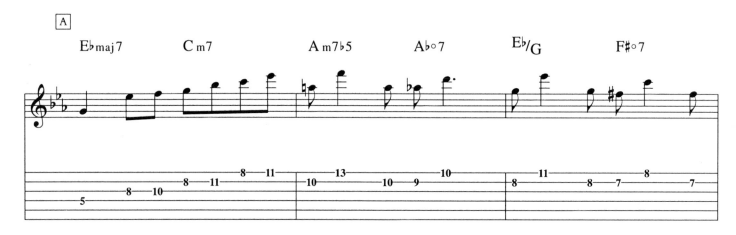

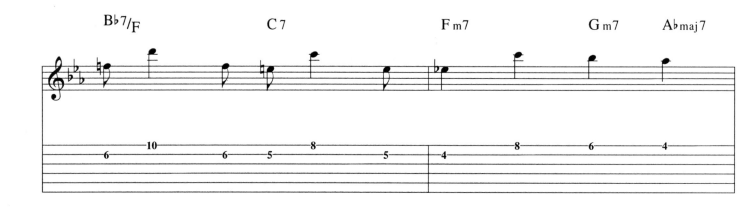

This page has been left blank to avoid awkward page turns.

Speak Low

Words by Ogden Nash
Music by Kurt Weill

Speak Low

(Chord Melody)

Arr. by Rick Stone

Words by Ogden Nash
Music by Kurt Weill

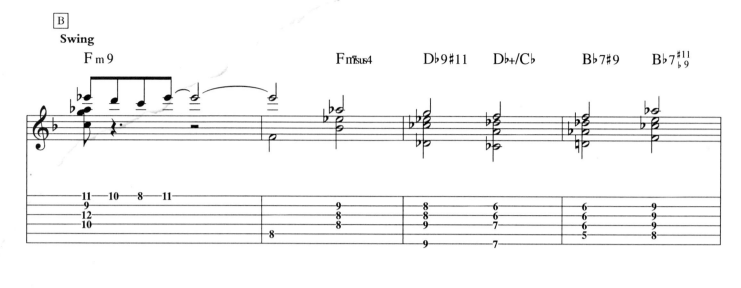

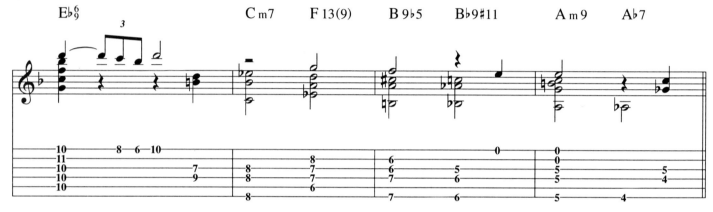

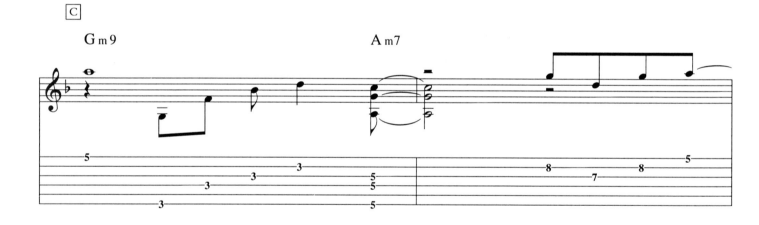

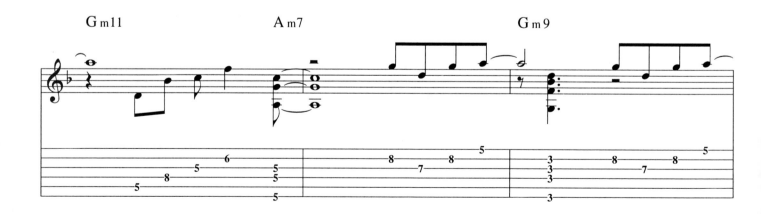

Speak Low

(Comping Etude)

Arr. by Rick Stone

Words by Ogden Nash
Music by Kurt Weill

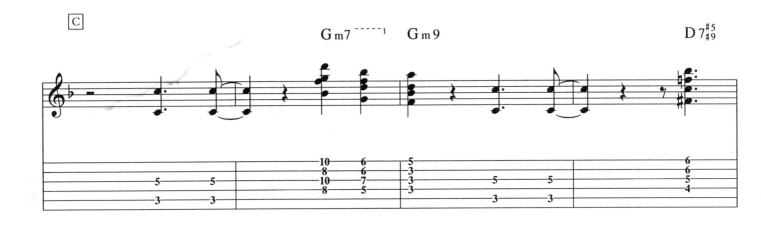

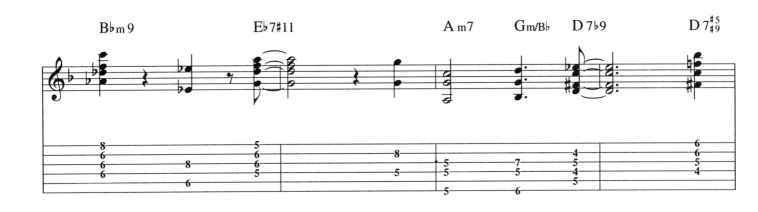

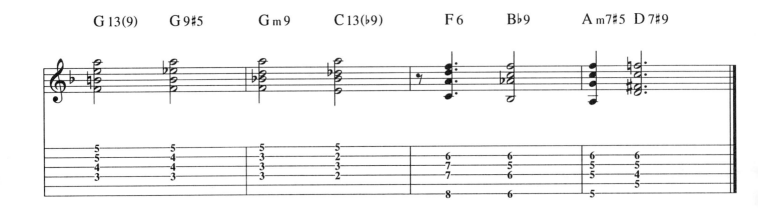

Speak Low
(Single-Note Solo)

Arr. by Rick Stone

Words by Ogden Nash
Music by Kurt Weill

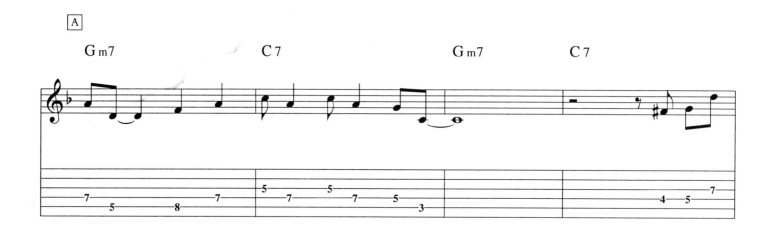

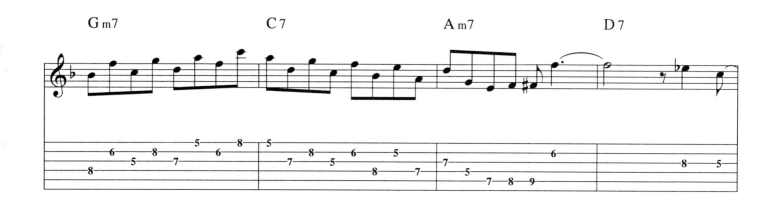

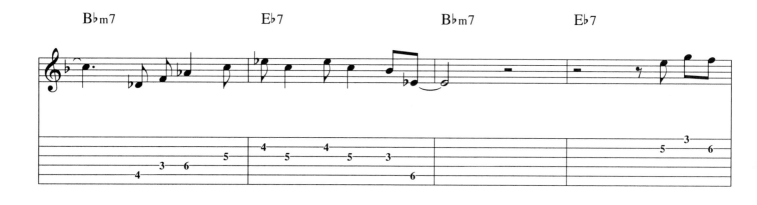

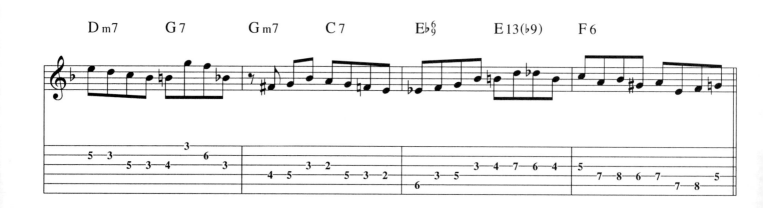

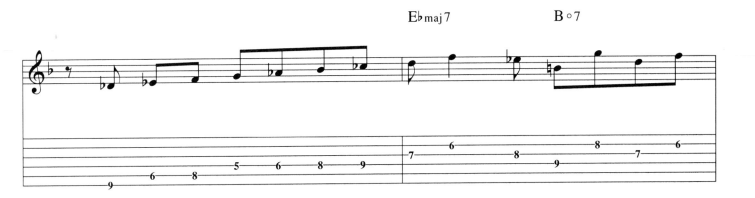

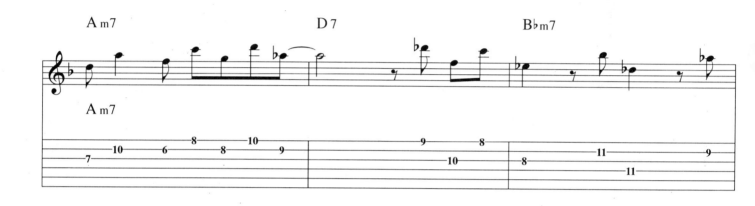

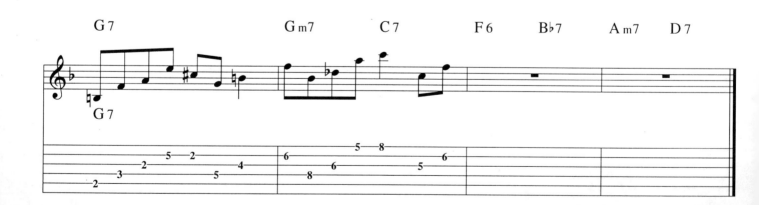

Summertime

By George Gershwin,
DuBose and Dorothy Heyward
and Ira Gershwin

Summertime

(Chord Melody)

Arr. by John C. Purse

By George Gershwin,
DuBose and Dorothy Heyward
and Ira Gershwin

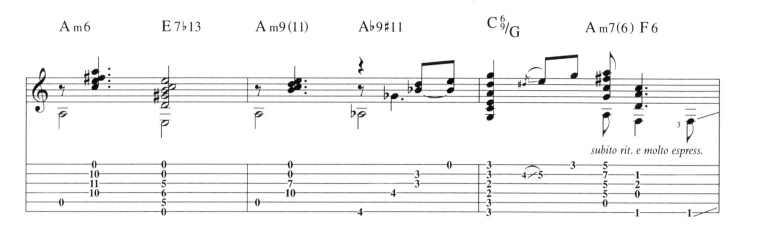

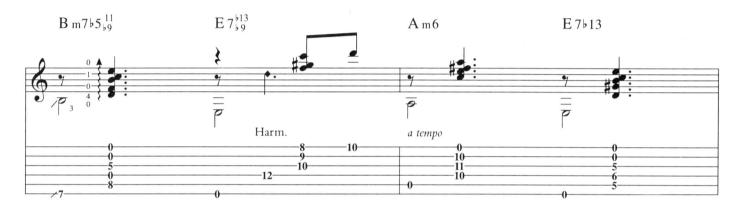

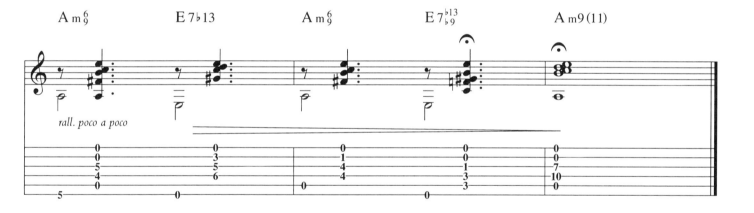

Summertime
(Comping Etude)

Arr. by John C. Purse

By George Gershwin,
DuBose and Dorothy Heyward
and Ira Gershwin

Summertime
(Single-Note Solo)

Arr. by John C. Purse

By George Gershwin,
DuBose and Dorothy Heyward
and Ira Gershwin

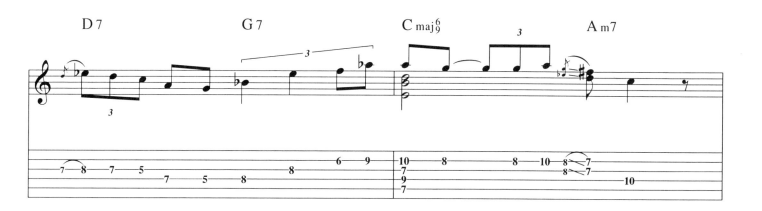

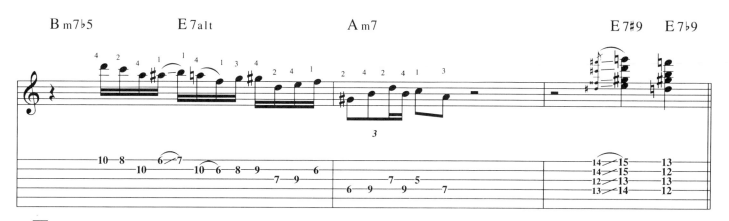

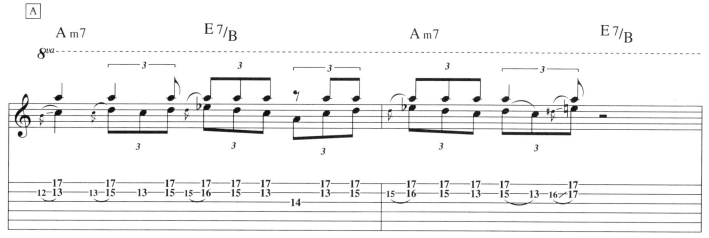

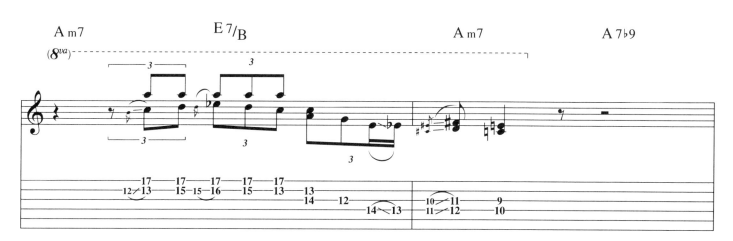

190

*This page has been
left blank to avoid
awkward page turns.*

THE WAY YOU LOOK TONIGHT

Words by DOROTHY FIELDS
Music by JEROME KERN

THE WAY YOU LOOK TONIGHT

Arr. by BRUCE SAUNDERS

(CHORD MELODY)

Words by DOROTHY FIELDS
Music by JEROME KERN

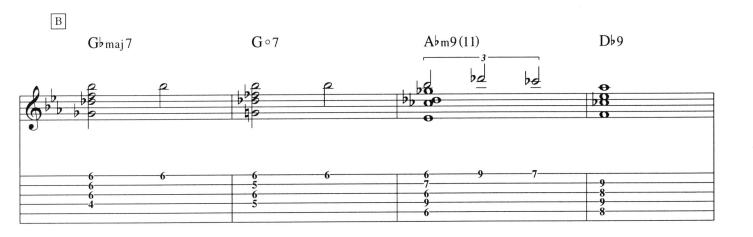

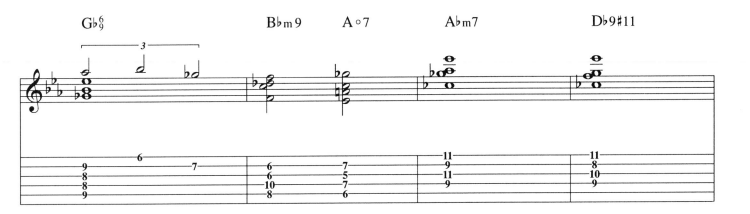

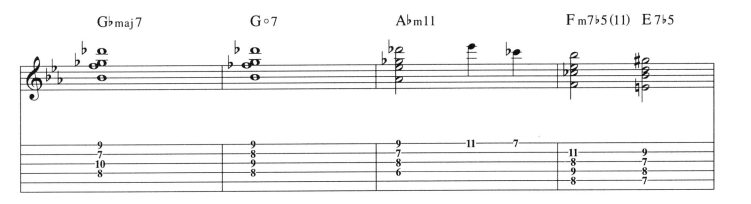

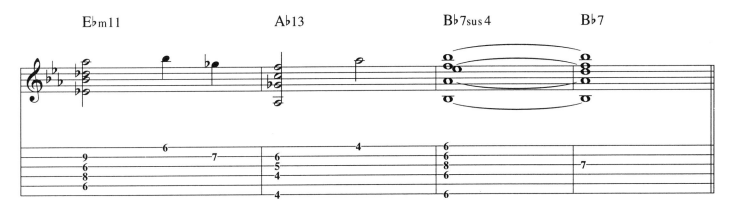

THE WAY YOU LOOK TONIGHT

Arr. by Bruce Saunders

(COMPING ETUDE)

Words by Dorothy Fields
Music by Jerome Kern

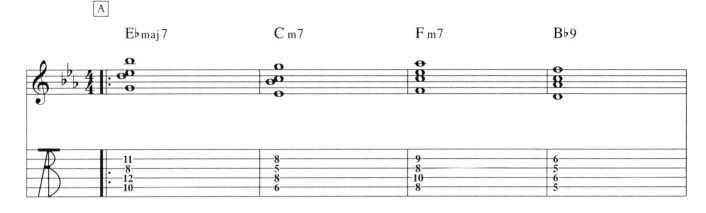

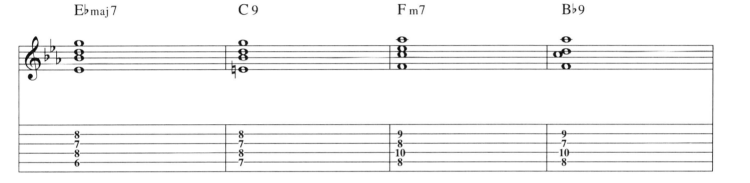

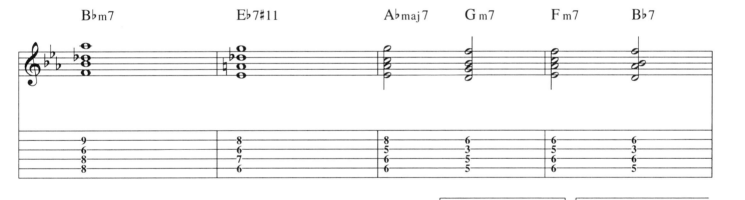

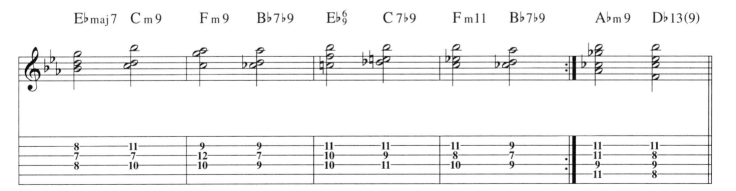

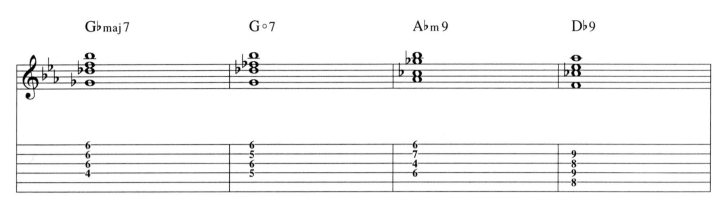

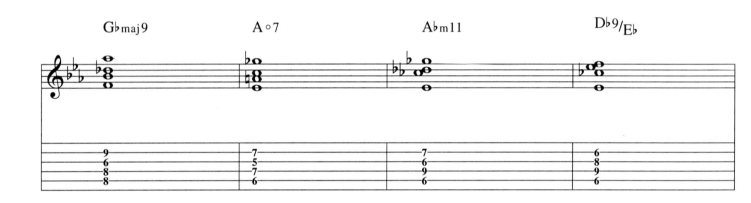

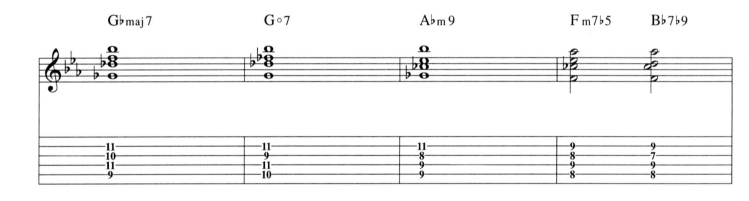

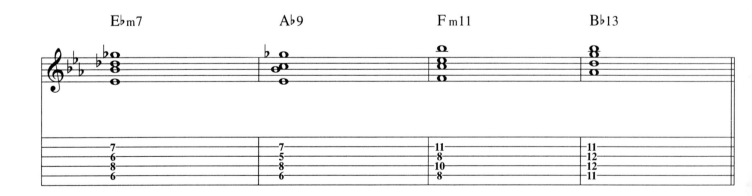

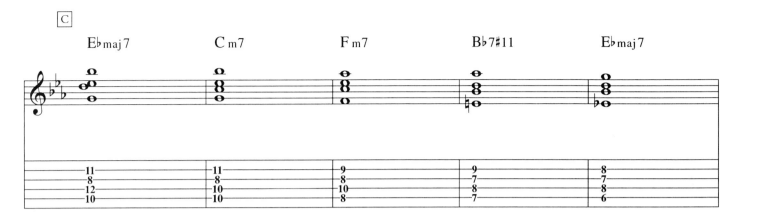

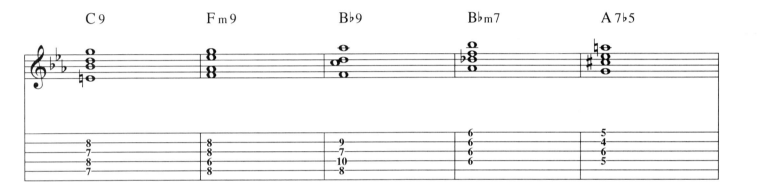

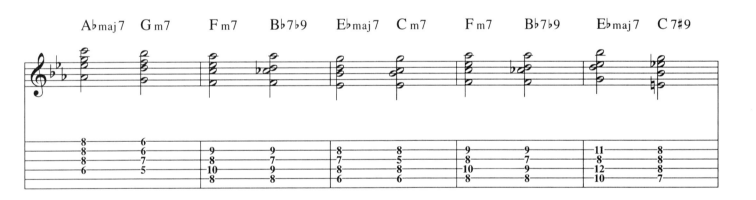

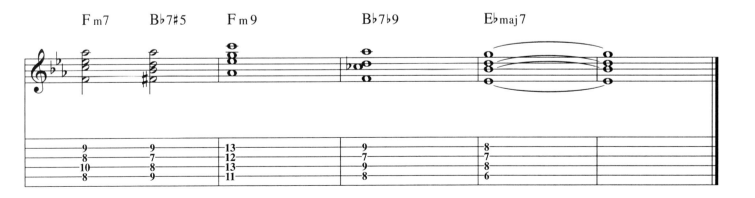

THE WAY YOU LOOK TONIGHT

(SINGLE-NOTE SOLO)

Arr. by BRUCE SAUNDERS

Words by DOROTHY FIELDS
Music by JEROME KERN

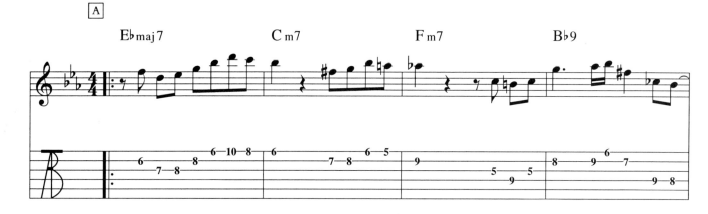

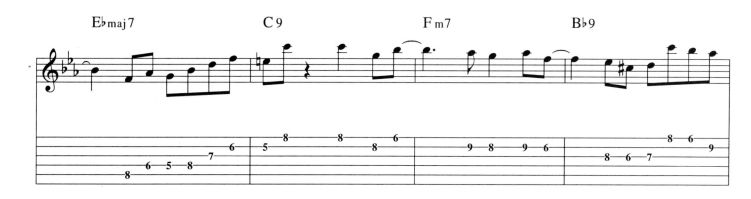

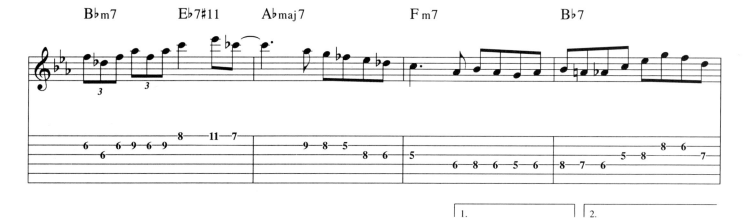

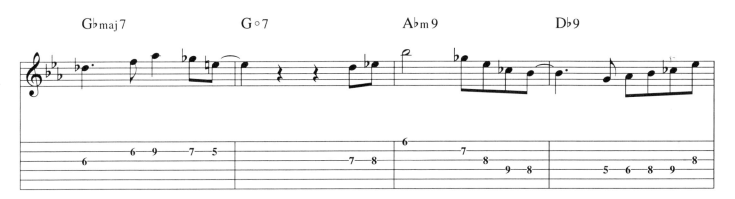

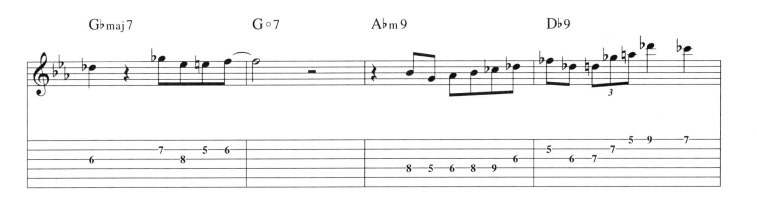

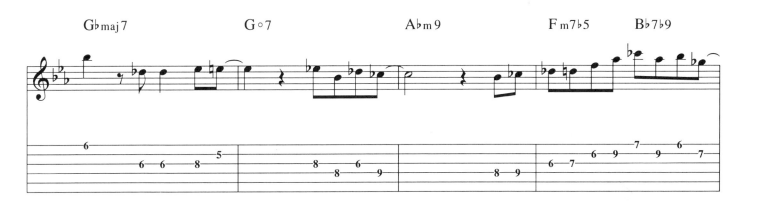

WHAT IS THIS THING CALLED LOVE?

Music and Lyrics by COLE PORTER

WHAT IS THIS THING CALLED LOVE?

Arr. by BRUCE SAUNDERS

(CHORD MELODY)

Music and Lyrics by COLE PORTER

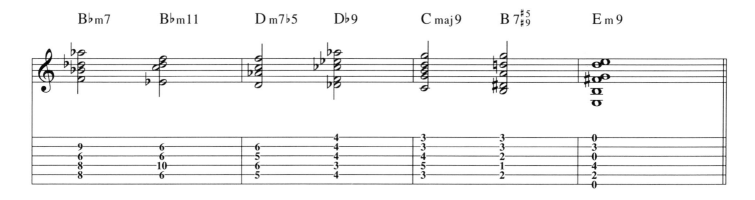

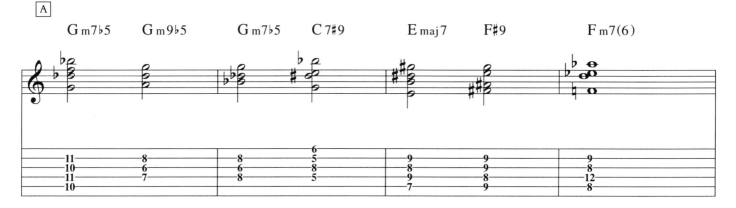

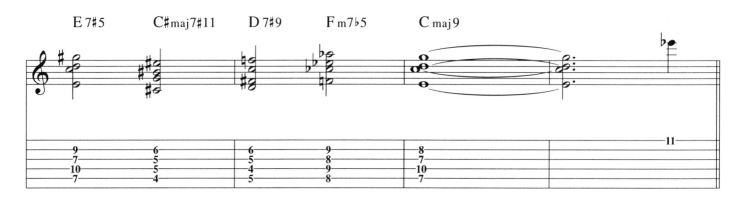

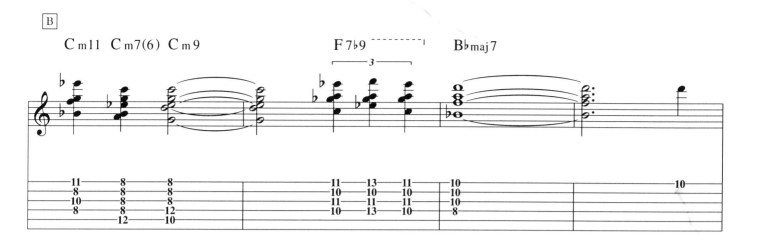

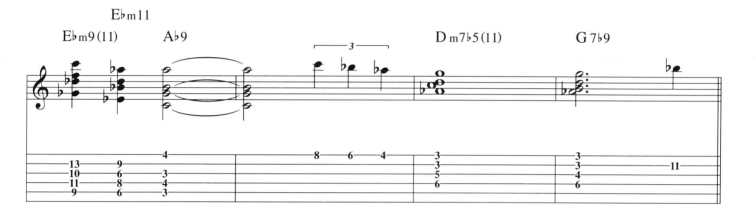

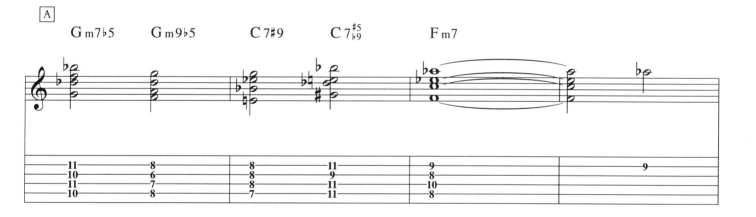

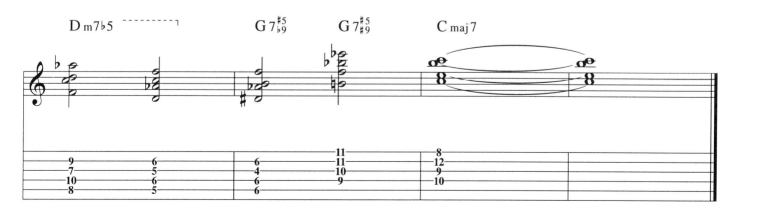

What Is This Thing Called Love?

Arr. by Bruce Saunders

(Comping Etude)

Music and Lyrics by Cole Porter

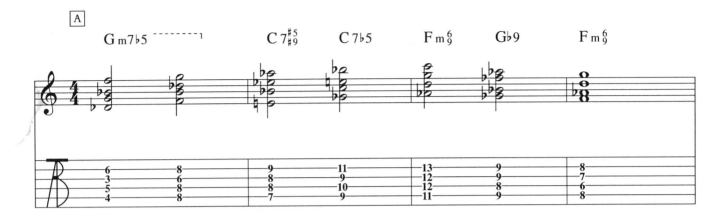

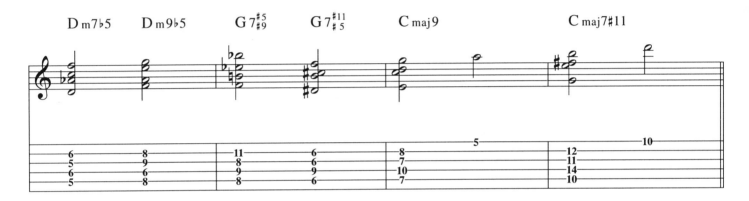

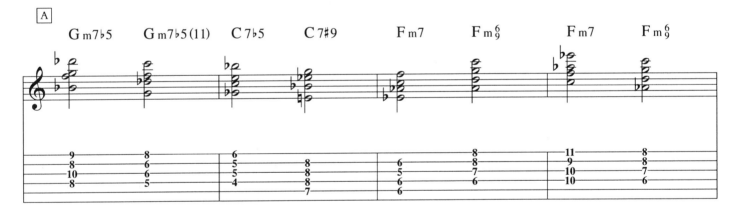

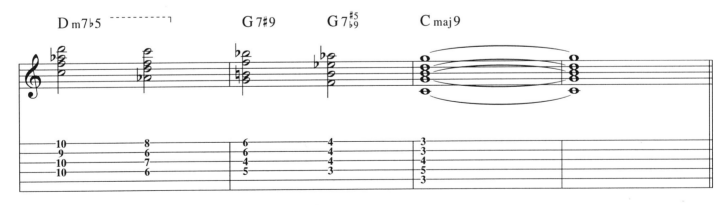

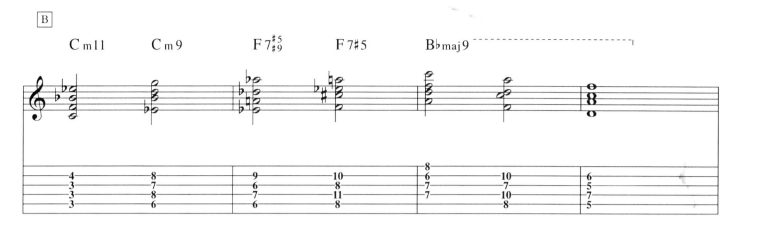

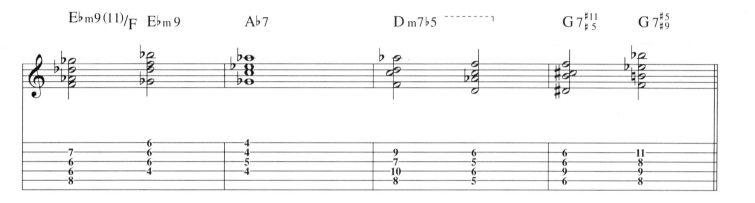

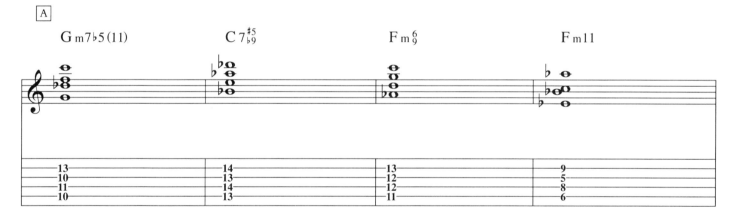

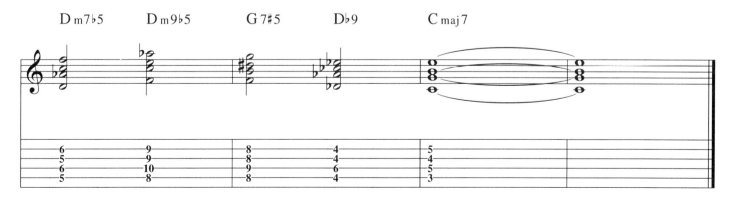

What Is This Thing Called Love?

Arr. by Bruce Saunders

(Single-Note Solo)

Music and Lyrics by Cole Porter

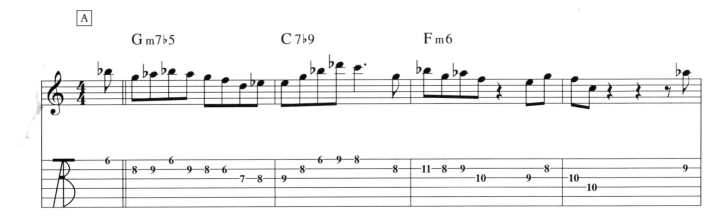

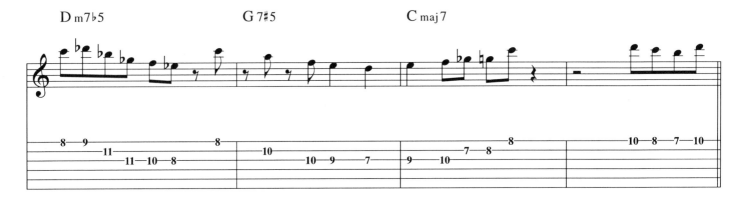

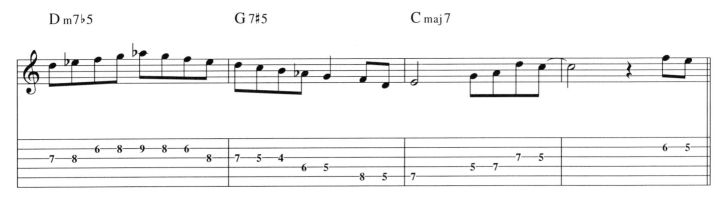

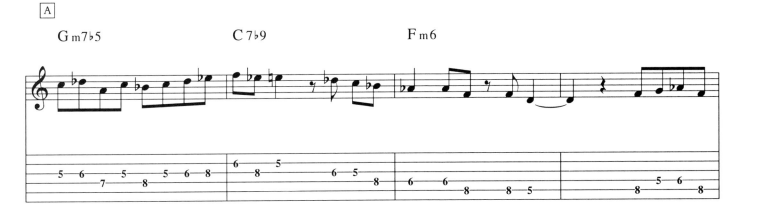

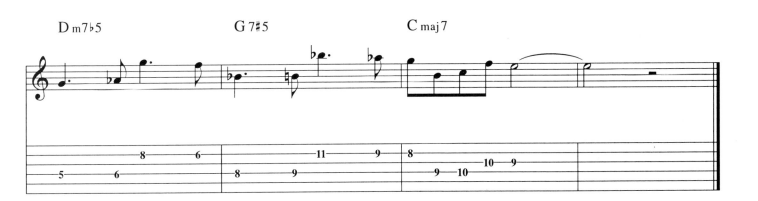

You Go To My Head

Words by HAVEN GILLESPIE
Music by J. FRED COOTS

You Go To My Head

Arr. by Sid Jacobs

(Chord Melody)

Words by Haven Gillespie
Music by J. Fred Coots

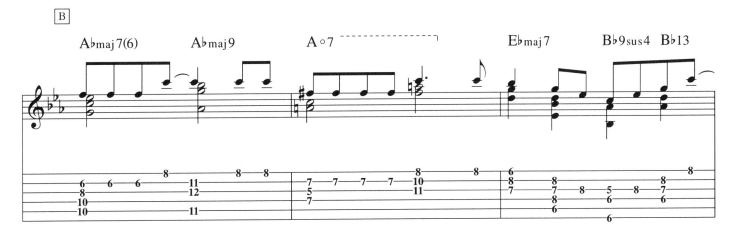

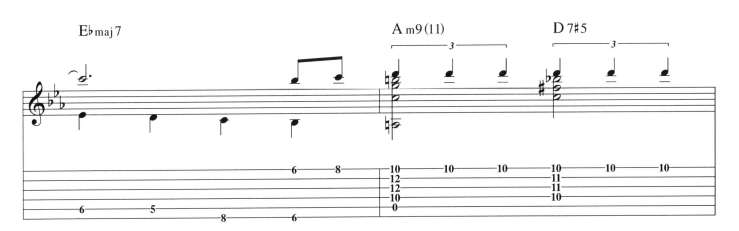

213

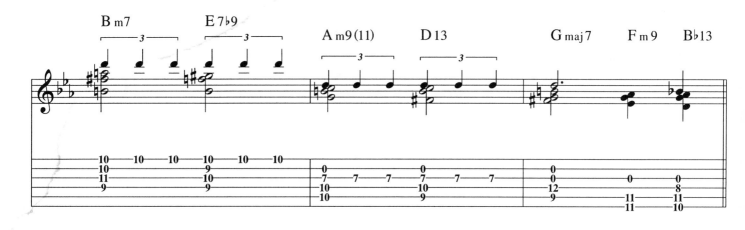

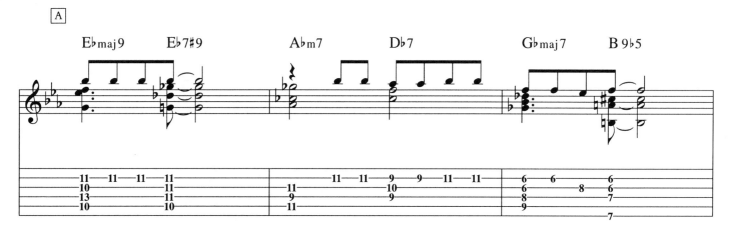

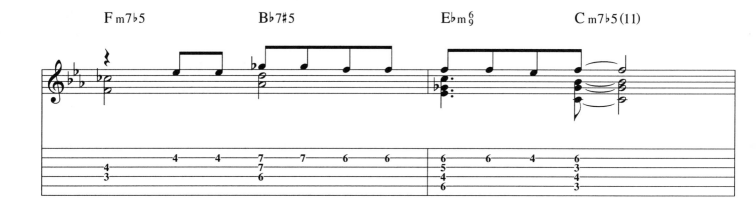

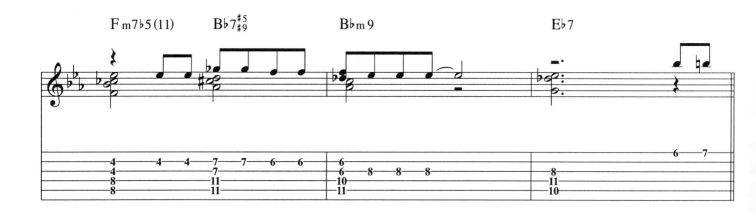

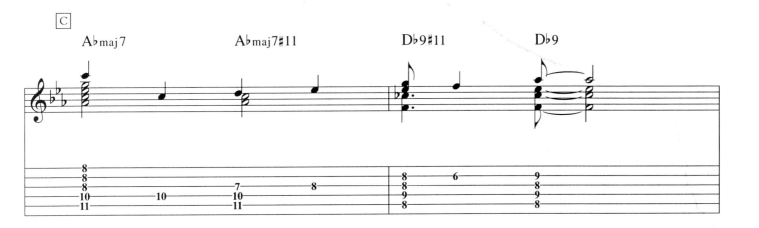

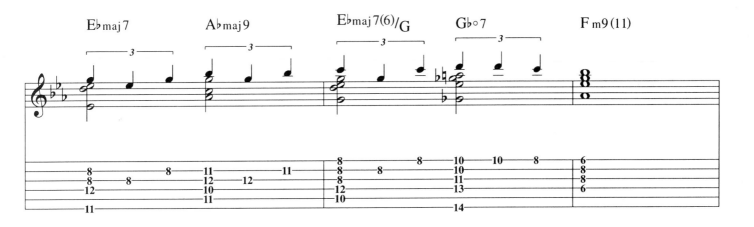

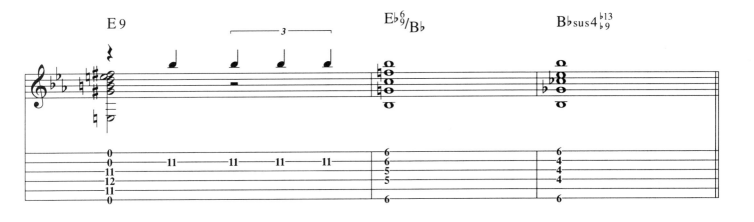

Outro

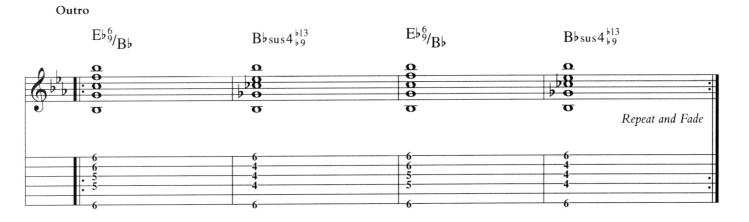

You Go To My Head

Arr. by Sid Jacobs

(Comping Etude)

Words by Haven Gillespie
Music by J. Fred Coots

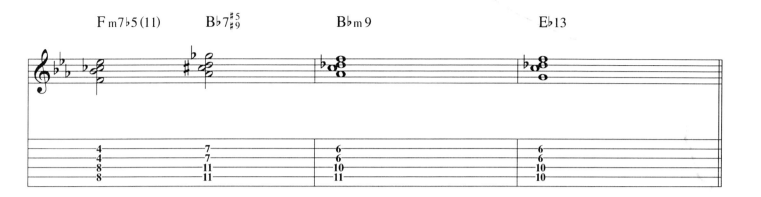

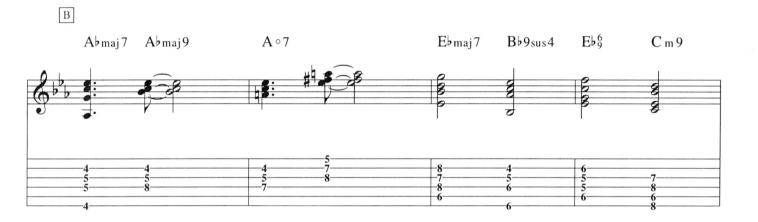

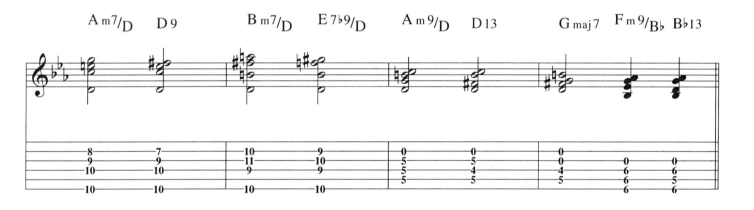

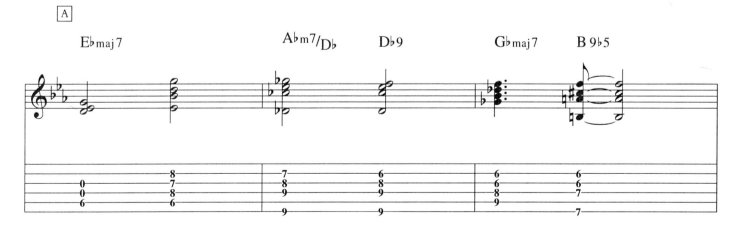

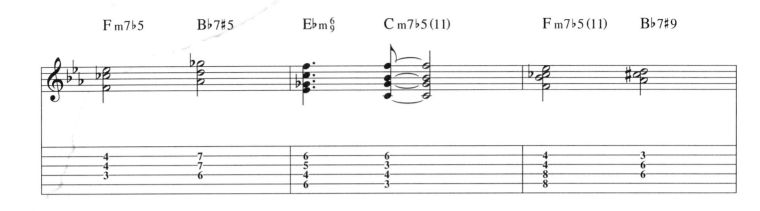

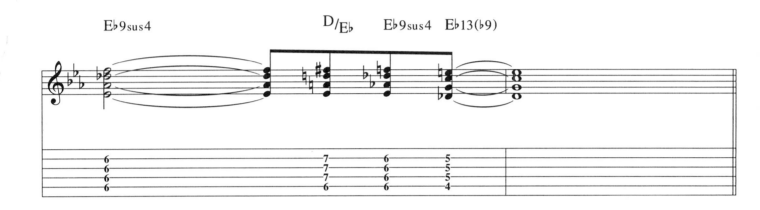

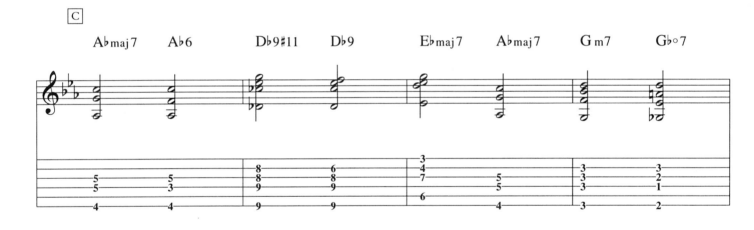

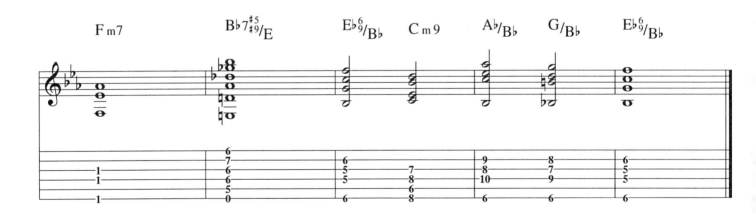

You Go To My Head
(Single-Note Solo)

Arr. by Sid Jacobs

Words by Haven Gillespie
Music by J. Fred Coots

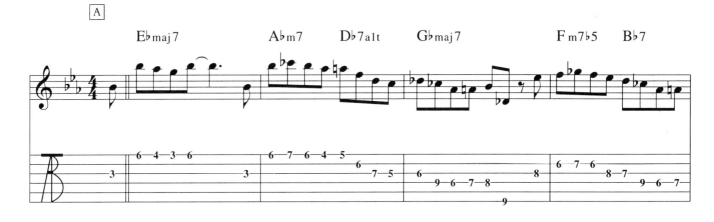

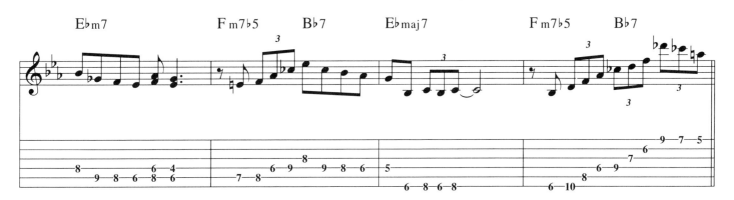

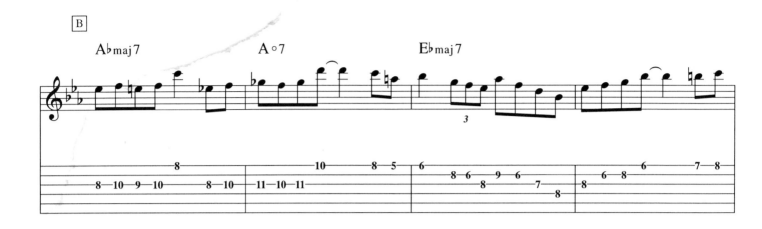

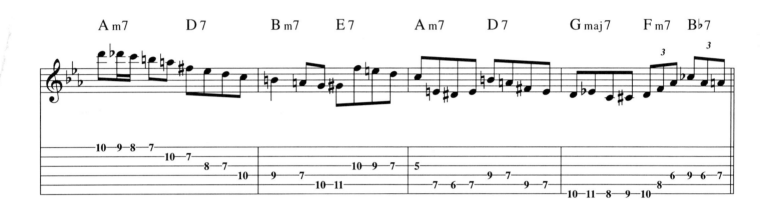

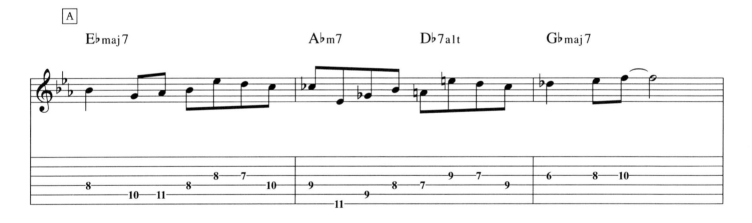

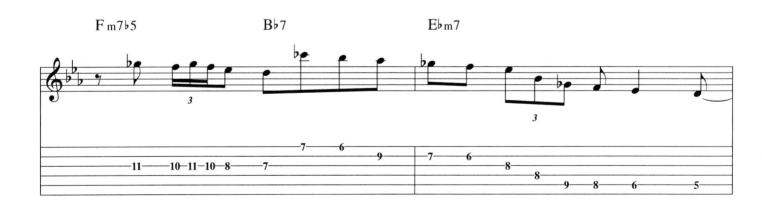

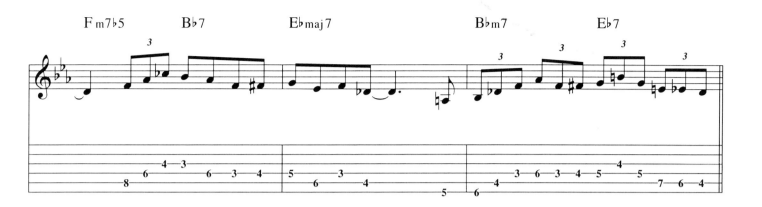

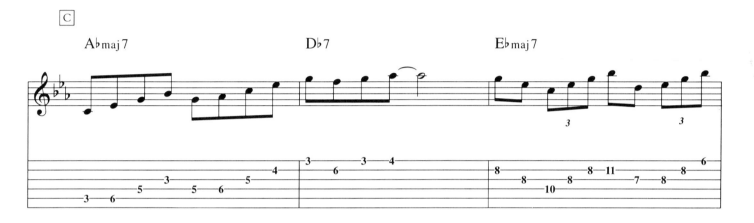

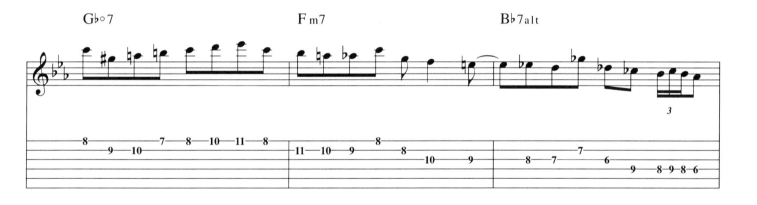

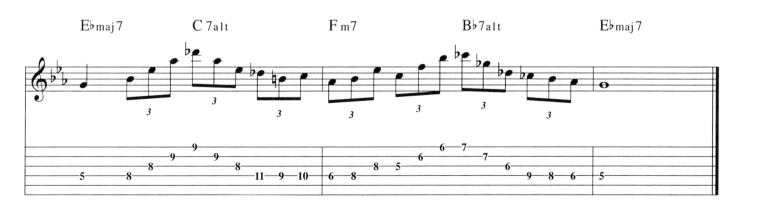

Arranger Index